"This book is a conduit for students, teachers, and teacher educators—a carefully guided path to making language learning not only possible, but meaningful and fun!"

—MARJORIE HALL HALEY, PHD, Board of Directors of the American Council on the Teaching of Foreign Languages, and Professor of Foreign/Second Language and English as a Second Language Education, George Mason University

"Many students with foreign-language learning difficulties have had long histories of trudging in the desert trying to learn a second language, an experience for which their learning differences often leave them ill equipped. Professor Konyndyk has developed a foreign-language instructional pedagogy that makes their deserts bloom. I think that students, foreign-language instructors, and special educators alike will find themselves grateful to her for this contribution."

—LYNN E. SNYDER, PHD, CCC-SLP, Professor Emerita and Former Director of the Center for Language and Learning, University of Colorado at Boulder

"Foreign-language educators, those in training to enter the field, and tutors will find this book an invaluable resource to meet struggling students' needs. A truly compassionate and experienced language specialist encourages us to integrate best practices that focus on each student's success while teaching excellent coping strategies. A long-awaited contribution to the field!"

—ELKE SCHNEIDER, PHD, College of Education, Winthrop University

"This teacher-friendly book offers a wide range of practical, research-based activities to help students with learning disabilities achieve success in foreign-language learning."

—LARRY VANDERGRIFT, PHD, former editor of the *Canadian Modern Language Review* and Professor Emeritus, Official Languages and Bilingualism Institute, University of Ottawa

D1506258

"*Foreign Languages for Everyone* is a must-have–must-read for all language teachers and language teacher trainers. We have struggled for too long without proper guidance, relying on either anecdotes from colleagues or dry research articles. This book reconciles research and application through the description of activities and strategies informed by research and tested in class by the author. This makes for a fascinating book where all language teachers, regardless of level and student population, can find something to reach all the students in their classes."

—ANNE VIOLIN-WIGENT, PHD, past president, Michigan World Language Association, Associate Professor of French, Michigan State University

Foreign Languages
for
EVERYONE

Foreign Languages
for
EVERYONE

How I Learned to Teach Second Languages
to Students with Learning Disabilities

Irene Brouwer Konyndyk

Forewords by
Lynn E. Snyder and Marjorie Hall Haley

edenridge press
GRAND RAPIDS, MICHIGAN

Copyright © 2011 by Irene Brouwer Konyndyk

Published by
Edenridge Press LLC
Grand Rapids, Michigan USA
www.edenridgepress.com
service@edenridgepress.com

All rights reserved. No part of this publication may be reproduced in any
form without permission from Edenridge Press LLC.

Quantity discount pricing is available.
service@edenridgepress.com
Fax: (616) 365-5797

Designed by Matthew Plescher
Edited by Quentin J. Schultze, Jean M. Blomquist, and Robert A. Banning

Konyndyk, Irene Brouwer
Foreign languages for everyone: how I learned to teach second languages to stu-
dents with learning disabilities / Irene Brouwer Konyndyk; forewords by Lynn E.
Snyder and Marjorie Hall Haley

ISBN-10 1937532909
ISBN-13 9781937532901 (alk. Paper)
Library of Congress Control Number: 2011944184

EDU029540 Education / Teaching Methods & Materials / Foreign Language
EDU026020 Education / Special Education / Learning Disabilities
EDU048000 Education / Inclusive Education

Printed in the United States of America

v2

To my daughter
Abigail Marissa Konyndyk

Contents

Foreword

by Lynn E. Snyder

IN THE SPRING OF 2000, Irene Konyndyk came to visit the Modified Foreign Language (MFL) Program at the University of Colorado at Boulder. My colleagues Doris Downey and Barbara Hill, authors of the MFL program's pedagogy, and I spent much of a day with her. From morning till night, we discussed our common passion: the needs of college students with foreign language learning difficulties and how best to teach them. We came away encouraged and fueled with her contagious enthusiasm.

Much has happened since that first meeting. Since then, Professor Konyndyk designed and implemented a successful MFL program in French, a language many colleagues considered too difficult for students with language-learning difficulties. In these last eleven years, she also honed her pedagogical principles and tools, broke new ground in metacognitive aspects of foreign-language pedagogy, engaged students with learning difficulties in the process of learning a foreign language, and changed their minds about themselves as learners and what they could accomplish. This book represents a synthesis of Professor Konyndyk's work in the classroom and in her discipline. In it, she shares a pedagogy that engages students who learn differently so that they can learn a foreign language and become independent self-teachers. This book debunks common misconceptions about students who struggle with foreign-language learning and exposes the flawed reasoning about their abilities. It is well titled; indeed, foreign languages are for everyone. Egalitarian, n'est-ce pas?

Much like the strong organization, structure, and strategies that Professor Konyndyk advocates in her pedagogy, this book is well organized and uses different forms of presentation. It also includes technology and offers, via her book-related website (www.foreignlanguagesforeveryone.com), an interactive forum for foreign-language instructors and special educators. This latter component is an important strength of this book. The inclusion of an interactive website and web access to materials makes it a growing, responsive, and self-updating instructional tool, not a volume that can become dated over time.

From a practical perspective, this book presents a variety of ways in which to engage students in learning the vocabulary, syntax, morphology, and culture of the language being taught. The learning strategies and foreign-language teaching activities are described in sufficient detail, with a number and variety of examples that allow us to replicate the activities with ease and/or modify them with clear intention. At the same time, the book is not a cookbook of activity recipes to be followed slavishly. Rather, it provides clear explanations of the educational and cognitive bases and rationale for these activities. This allows instructors to alter the activities to meet students' needs without sacrificing the integrity of the learning process. In the fall of 2004, I had the opportunity to participate in some of these activities firsthand in one of Professor Konyndyk's MFL classes. I can personally attest to an engaging, interactive, and enjoyable experience. I had no idea how much of my high school and college French could be reactivated after so many years!

One of the strongest contributions of this book, and perhaps one of Professor Konyndyk's unique contributions to the literature, is her development of the metacognitive component for foreign-language instruction. Its strength seems to lie in the ways in which she sensitizes students to their own learning strategies, her use of student journals, and her own learning perspective as she responds to them. She uses quotes taken from student journal entries throughout the book to support and/or illustrate specific points she makes, especially about their growing metacognitive awareness. I found the journal entries candid, transparent, and balanced. More importantly, her development of the student journal experience and the integral role it plays in student learning relays a strong message to both teachers and students about the students' self-worth.

As I finished reading *Foreign Languages for Everyone*, I tried to see if I could identify the keys to Professor Konyndyk's approach to foreign language learning. I found that two underlying operating principles seem to permeate the pedagogy described in this book and the very nature of Professor Konyndyk herself: respect for students and their self-worth and the role of grace, or unmerited favor, in the learning process. These principles, obviously, reflect benchmarks of her faith. I must say that it edifies me, challenges me, encourages me, and fills me with gratitude that she has written this volume.

C. S. Lewis once wrote, "The task of the modern educator is not to cut down jungles, but to irrigate deserts." Many students with foreign-language learning difficulties have had long histories of trudging in the desert trying to learn a second language, an experience for which their learning differences often leave them ill equipped. Professor Konyndyk has developed a foreign-language instructional pedagogy that makes their deserts bloom. I think that students, foreign-language instructors, and special educators alike will find themselves grateful to her for this contribution.

Lynn E. Snyder, PhD, CCC-SLP, is Professor Emerita and former Director of the Center for Language and Learning, University of Colorado at Boulder.

Foreword

by Marjorie Hall Haley

IT IS WITH GREAT PLEASURE that I write a foreword to this book, *Foreign Languages for Everyone*. The topic is timely and overdue for our profession; it is necessary for us to be able to read in very plain language how to address the needs of diverse learners, that is, students who learn differently. Over the last decade, my own research has centered on accommodating learner differences and how to provide optimal learning conditions. One size does not fit all, and teachers, administrators, and teacher educators must readily acquiesce that one lesson plan no longer suffices for that entire sea of faces in today's classrooms. Today's millennial learners come to our classrooms having been educated in a technologically driven era. Most learners are fully aware of "how" they learn best, and some even demand that they be taught accordingly. The paradigm shift has occurred to such a degree that we no longer assume the apex position in a teacher-centered classroom, but rather the focus is directed toward learner-centered, discovery learning, and/or learning by doing.

Oftentimes we encounter research literature in language education focused on the theoretical and not the practical. A large proportion of published material springs from faculty and academic professionals removed from clinical settings, and I have found that to be of little use to practitioners in the field. Dr. Irene Brouwer Konyndyk is a teachers' teacher. She understands and demonstrates empathy for students who may have had limited prior access to foreign language study and/or limited success in a language learning environment. This book is a conduit for students, teachers, and teacher educators—a carefully guided path to making language learning not only possible but also meaningful and fun!

The ideas and strategies listed in this book are step by step and easy to follow. The book is appropriate for both pre- and in-service teachers who may be struggling with understanding how to meet the needs of students who learn differently. The resources are rich and grounded in research. Teachers can pick this book up at any given chapter and find useful information for specific areas of concern.

As a teacher educator in a large public urban university, I find that most of our graduates who interview for their first teaching job are asked three simple questions: (1) How well do you know the target language? (2) What do you know about classroom management? (3) How do you plan to teach diverse learners? This book will provide a wonderful resource to both novice and veteran teachers who are looking for easy-to-read suggestions provided by someone who has shared her wealth of teaching, learning, and living experiences.

Acknowledging that students learn differently can be daunting. Teachers are expected to provide language instruction that includes standards-based, research-solid, and differentiated instruction for all learners. Education reform has become a top priority in the United States. Educators who respect their students' own developmental learning skills and strategies will find Konyndyk's book, *Foreign Languages for Everyone*, immensely rewarding. Dr. Konyndyk gives us rich accounts and examples of ways to reach and teach students "where they are" when they come to us. She does not suggest that we force all students into a cookie-cutter approach to learning and/or acquiring new languages.

Throughout the book, Dr. Konyndyk demonstrates a love of teaching and learning and her compassionate desire to make multilingualism available to all. Her work is kind, generous, and caring for both teacher and student. Her spirited defense of learner differences is admirable, as is Konyndyk's defense of the interests of all language learners.

Marjorie Hall Haley, PhD, serves on the Board of Directors of the American Council on the Teaching of Foreign Languages (ACTFL). She is also Professor of Foreign/Second Language and English as a Second Language Education, Director of Foreign Language Teacher Licensure, Graduate School of Education, George Mason University.

Preface

THIS BOOK IS ABOUT HOW I LEARNED to teach a second language to those who either have failed before or were not really given a chance to succeed. I wrote it to help others to be smart, productive teachers of foreign languages to students with learning disabilities. In a sense, the book called me. My life journey prepared and inspired me to write it.

When I began teaching languages in the 1970s, first as a graduate assistant, then as a high school instructor, and finally as a college professor, I encountered many bright and even academically accomplished students who struggled to learn a second language. I really didn't understand why they couldn't succeed. Was it my teaching? Was it their learning?

I had been born in the Netherlands and later learned English. I learned another language, so why couldn't everyone—if they really wanted to? My students had learned their first language. What was *their* problem? Maybe they just needed to work a little harder. Or maybe I needed to learn how to teach them differently.

Looking back on my own learning experiences, I had to admit being better at languages than science. I eagerly began learning French in ninth grade, added Latin in tenth grade, and German a year later—studying all three languages simultaneously my last two years of secondary school. By contrast, math and science were not so easy for me. I didn't enjoy them either. But in college, I had to take courses in math and physics. So I decided to "get them out of the way" early in my program—only to discover later that those two courses were no longer required of students like me who had completed four years of science and math in high school. It seemed unfair. But the experience with math and science helped me empathize with students who have difficulty learning a subject. I couldn't say that every struggling second-language learner was lazy, disorganized, or dumb. There had to be more to the story.

I continued to encounter struggling students, many of whom were sent to a learning-disabilities coordinator for testing, deemed to have "X" (usually an auditory processing weakness), and given a language-requirement waiver or substitution. I'd ask the school's learning-disabilities office to tell me how to teach students with "X," but I never received a satisfactory answer. I was frustrated. So I decided to determine on my own how to help them learn. Someone had to know the secret! I soon discovered wonderful research related to foreign-language learning as well as learning disabilities. But most of it was written by learning-disabilities scholars examining native-language acquisition. I'd have to figure out on my own how to apply it to teaching a foreign language.

Along the way, my desire to help struggling learners turned personal. One of my own children began having learning difficulties. She was very intelligent, but didn't learn like her siblings. For instance, she struggled with reading and memorizing. By experimenting, she and I figured out that she could memorize much better by adding rhythm and body motions to lyrics; a multisensory approach somehow helped her to embed language into her brain. My husband and I also noticed that she easily got frustrated playing the piano, although less so than her helpful father! She didn't seem to understand how the various notes on the page related to the keys on the piano.

On the other hand, our daughter learned as a young child how to knock a softball into the outfield. She interacted intuitively with people—as if she had a built-in sense of how to connect with others. Given her talents, I wondered what was going on inside her brain that made some kinds of learning so difficult. What were my husband and I missing? Testing ultimately indicated that she had difficulties with attention and memory. Nevertheless, she eventually earned a master's degree from a prestigious university. But in between her childhood and adulthood were years of learning—for her and for me. She taught me a lot about the perplexing

* see resource at www.foreignlanguagesforeveryone.com

but wonderfully amazing differences among learners. She gave me much hope in my own abilities as a teacher-learner. I'm honored to dedicate this book to the daughter who helped propel me on my journey of learning how to teach at-risk students.

These four strands of my life—seeking to teach a second language to all students, struggling myself with math and science, studying the literature about language-learning difficulties, and learning from my own daughter—came together for me in the late 1990s when I felt called to develop a pedagogical approach that would meet the needs of at-risk students. I asked my institution (Calvin College in Grand Rapids, Michigan) for support to develop a course sequence that employed a methodology that was multisensory, highly structured, and significantly metacognitive. I received permission to run a three-year pilot program in 2001. It proved highly successful. The three-course sequence is now a regular offering in the college's liberal arts curriculum. Students must take particular steps* in order to be admitted into my modified foreign-language program.

What is it like to teach in this program? Here's a note I found in my mailbox at the end of one academic year:

> As my college career is coming to a close, there have been few people who I feel have made a significant impact on my life. . . . I cannot thank you enough for the . . . unconditional care you showed to me and all the other students. . . . Though I was told for such a long time "No, you can't," you constantly were a voice saying "Yes, you can and you will." You not only helped show me that the world of language is one that is possible for me, but you also showed me the way that we as Christians can have such a positive impact on the lives of others.

That note reminds me how important it is to see the capacity in my students as I teach them a foreign language. I'm blessed to teach those who struggle to learn a second language. Some would call my students "at risk" or "learning disabled." But they're also smart. I never knew how smart such at-risk students are until I became smart enough to teach them as uniquely talented individuals.

Over the years, I've shared my knowledge and expertise with colleagues at conferences in the foreign-language and learning-disabilities communities in Canada, the United States, and Europe.* I've also published several articles and taught a weeklong graduate workshop on the topic.* But I always knew that in order for my effective practices to more fully serve the second-language learning community, I needed to write a book that would bridge the gap between the foreign-language and learning-disabilities worlds and serve as a more permanent and practical resource for others. This is that book. Now I present it to you with humility, gratitude, and delight.

—IRENE BROUWER KONYNDYK,
October 2011

Note: When asterisks appear in the text, they indicate that the material mentioned can be found on my website, www.foreignlanguagesforeveryone.com.

* see resource at www.foreignlanguagesforeveryone.com

Acknowledgments

I OWE MUCH TO MANY PEOPLE. First, I thank my wonderful students, especially those in my multisensory foreign-language program at Calvin College. They taught me a great deal about perseverance, individual uniqueness, and the joy of community.

I'm grateful for my foreign-language colleagues and the administration at Calvin College for their encouragement and support—heartening me to move forward on my convictions, test my ideas, and bring this book to fruition. The college awarded me a sabbatical, college research fellowships, and a McGregor Fellowship. In addition, I thank Karen Broekstra, head of Student Services at Calvin College, for unrelentingly advocating for at-risk students. I also owe a debt of thanks to my students in a graduate workshop at Calvin College during the summer of 2010, who read the main chapters of my manuscript as their course text and gave me much helpful feedback, especially Spanish examples.

I'm very grateful to Lynn E. Snyder of the University of Colorado, who kindly taught me about their fine program and with whom I submitted a grant proposal to the Fund for the Improvement of Postsecondary Education. Lynn believed in my work and encouraged me along the way.

I thank Leonore Ganschow and Elke Schneider, who led workshops at Calvin College. Their work, along with that of Richard L. Sparks, launched the personal journey I describe in this book.

I am indebted to Quentin Schultze, who helped make this a reader-friendly book.

I also want to express my deep gratitude and love to my husband, Roger Dale Konyndyk, for standing firmly beside me, always listening to my stories of the day and faithfully encouraging me in everything I have felt called to do.

Finally, I want to thank my daughter, Abigail Marissa Konyndyk, for showing me in a real and tangible way how each person, created *imago Dei*, has both strengths and weaknesses and that, paradoxically, our Creator performs something wonderful in each of us. I'm honored to dedicate this book to her.

I love the metaphor of a tapestry—our lives are made up of so many different threads. From the underside we see the knots, the flaws, the brokenness, but from the top God sees a wonderful story that sparkles with golden color and life. *Soli Deo Gloria.*

Introduction

*Reaching Out to Our Struggling
Second-Language Learners*

When I was a little girl in Canada, my Dutch-immigrant father would ask people on the phone, "Is it that you are going to be home tomorrow?" It seemed like awkward phrasing to my young mind. Although I was born in the Netherlands and lived there until the age of four, I had been growing up learning English. He had grown up with a very different native language and culture. We dwelled in the same North American land, but our minds inhabited different linguistic worlds. Eventually I understood that the way my father frequently asked questions in English was his way of avoiding the complicated inversion of subject and verb: "Are you going to be home tomorrow?"

Everyone who learns a second language is like an immigrant arriving in a new, already inhabited land that initially seems far too complicated to dwell in comfortably. Foreign-language students, too, embark on a journey into the collective mind of another culture. Moreover, students make the journey with their own educational, cultural, and biological backgrounds. Each student is different—unique. We foreign-language teachers are unique too. Yet we dwell for a time in the same classroom with our unique students so we can help each other make the journey. We educators are like tour guides with a busload of very different individuals from all kinds of different neighborhoods. When we meet with our students for class, we invite them to get off the bus with us and check out the foreign neighborhood.

Some of the students who join us on the journey bring along truly remarkable experiences. They include at-risk students who may have struggled with formal learning their entire lives. Often they are among the smartest students in our classrooms. But sometimes no teachers have told them that, because the teachers themselves were ill equipped to identify the students' unique learning abilities. When these at-risk students enter a foreign-language classroom, they face special challenges that very few educators have been trained to identify and address. So we teachers are understandably at a loss about how to serve such student-immigrants entering a foreign land of inverted queries and incomprehensible sounds. The easiest thing is simply for educators to waive language requirements and pretend that such students can't make the journey successfully. We kindly invite such students to leave the bus. Their tour is over. Chances are they will live the rest of their lives at home, feeling they are incapable of learning a foreign language and never again having the opportunity to dwell in another culture.

As I explained in the preface, I have learned both personally and professionally that just about every at-risk student should be on the foreign-language journey with us. At-risk students can nearly all learn a foreign language and enjoy a second culture. That's why I wrote this book. Nothing that I have done in my professional life as a teacher of elementary, secondary, and college students has given me more satisfaction than teaching a foreign language to at-risk students. I invite you to get on the bus with me and my students for the journey through the pages of this book. I'll be your guide into the minds and hearts of anxious at-risk students who never thought that they could learn a second language—and might have even failed to do so previously. I'll share with you how my students taught me to teach them. I'll share my students' personal journal entries about what a difference learning a second language and culture has meant to them personally and academically. I'll give you the practical tools and pedagogical insights that will help you successfully teach a second language to students with various types of learning disabilities.

The need is great. More and more students with learning disabilities have been mainstreamed into regular classrooms in K–12 schools, colleges, and foreign-language classrooms.[1] This includes students on the autism spectrum, such as those with Asperger's syndrome. As more schools see the importance of introducing children to foreign languages at a younger age, and as many states change their high school graduation requirements to include several years of foreign-language study, anxiety grows about how at-risk students will fare. Parents understandably worry whether a child struggling to read in English is going to be able to acquire another language. Meanwhile, foreign-language teachers often lack training in recognizing and meeting the needs of at-risk students. Learning-disabilities specialists know little about how foreign languages are taught. The result is poor collaboration between the learning-disabilities service providers and the foreign-language community.[2] This book explains how I learned—with the help of my students, colleagues, and the academic literature—to bridge that gap.

Changing How We Teach

Changes in foreign-language teaching methods have also made things more difficult for at-risk students, whose needs are finally being recognized. The current approach—the "natural" or "communicative" method—generally works well for traditional students. But it's not very effective for struggling learners.[3] If you were taught to teach using natural-language methods, please don't assume that you would have a difficult time switching to an alternative pedagogy. I made the switch, and you can too. The key is understanding how at-risk students learn—and then adapting our teaching to their learning. In one sense, the purpose of this book is to help you learn how to teach students who simply learn differently. Once you understand how at-risk students learn, you can adapt your own lesson plans to maximize their comprehension, retention, and performance of a second language.

Defining Learning Disabilities

Since in this book I focus on learning disabilities rather than physical disabilities, I need to begin by defining "learning disability." Of course, there are many definitions.[4] I use the one articulated by the National Joint Committee on Learning Disabilities (NJCLD):

> Learning disabilities is a general term that refers to a heterogeneous group of disorders manifested by significant difficulties in the acquisition and use of listening, speaking, reading, writing, reasoning, or mathematical abilities. These disorders are intrinsic to the individual, presumed to be due to central nervous system dysfunction, and may occur across the life span. Problems in self-regulatory behaviors, social perception,

and social interaction may exist with learning disabilities but do not by themselves constitute a learning disability. Although learning disabilities may occur concomitantly with other handicapping conditions (for example, sensory impairment, mental retardation, serious emotional disturbance), or with extrinsic influences (such as cultural differences, insufficient or inappropriate instruction), they are not the result of those conditions or influences.[5]

Clearly the primary areas of difficulty are directly related to language—especially listening, speaking, reading, and writing. So the connection between native-language learning difficulties and foreign-language learning is understandable. Since foreign-language difficulties are based on native-language difficulties, students who struggle with grammatical concepts in English generally struggle with target-language grammar. Leading scholars in the study of foreign-language learning and learning disabilities support this linguistic connection.[6]

Identifying Our At-Risk Students

How do your students hold their writing instruments? Have you ever received a student's handwritten assignment that curled up at the edges?* In forming the letters on the page, did the student press so hard that the letters showed through on the back side? Imagine the effort that went into writing such a page! But also consider the fact that such writing might be a sign of "dysgraphia"—when even copying words takes extreme concentration, and holding a pen or pencil is often awkward.

From my own observations and the literature, I realized that students exhibit various difficulties that affect their learning. These difficulties lie on a severity continuum and include attention difficulties, memory difficulties, brain injury–related difficulties, organizational difficulties, and emotional disorders, such as clinical depression or obsessive-compulsive disorder (OCD). For example, suppose you observe a student carefully emptying a bag of candies, sorting them by color, organizing them into rows, and then eating them one entire row at a time. Does that student perhaps suffer with OCD? How would you know? What difference would it make in how you teach? Our job as educators isn't to make clinical diagnoses. But we can

* see resource at www.foreignlanguagesforeveryone.com

be better teachers when we pay attention to students, learn about various disorders and difficulties, collaborate with other professionals, and do our best to work with our learners as distinct persons.

In my experience, at-risk students commonly display one or more of the following issues in English (assuming English is their native language):

- Punctuating and spelling improperly
- Spacing words on a page irregularly*
- Employing verb tenses confusingly
- Misusing prepositions

According to scholars at the University of Colorado, additional areas of difficulty include these:

- Falling behind quickly
- Missing part of what is said in the classroom
- Needing information repeated
- Having very short memory
- Being anxious and tending to "blank out"
- Demonstrating inconsistent quality of work
- Being unable to listen and take notes simultaneously
- Being disorganized with class work, academic work, and personal life
- Being unsure how to study
- Studying for hours and still failing
- Appearing to not pay attention in class
- Working hard with poor results
- Feeling extreme frustration

Yet the same students can demonstrate remarkable strengths and talents. Many students struggle because they have been subjected to a Western educational system where reading, spelling, and on-paper activities are the norm, where organization is prized, and where standardized tests determine success and admission to prestigious educational programs. These students don't typically get to shine in the areas where their talents lie: creativity, problem solving, intuitiveness, and hands-on activities—to name just a few. Nevertheless, after suffering their way through the educational system, they frequently become business leaders, entrepreneurs, artists, dancers, musicians, engineers, architects, designers, and software developers. They tend to be highly inventive individuals who truly think innovatively. They're the Leonardo da Vincis, the Albert Einsteins, and the Temple Grandins of the world. We need them for the benefit of humankind.

Reviewing Second-Language Research

A vast body of literature exists on the struggles of students with learning disabilities in foreign-language learning, ranging from difficulties with phonology, semantics, or syntax, to the affective domain (anxiety, motivation, etc.).[7] Some students find foreign-language learning an almost insurmountable hurdle; others are steered away from language learning. Countless students really want to learn a foreign language but are deprived of its numerous, rich benefits—and the sheer fun of encountering another culture's way of experiencing life.

Richard L. Sparks and Leonore Ganschow, two of the leading scholars in the field, developed the linguistic coding differences hypothesis to understand why some students seem to struggle in a foreign-language classroom.[8] Sparks found no differences between students diagnosed with a learning disability and those who struggle but have no documentation.[9] He contends that all students should be given the opportunity to learn a foreign language rather than being given waivers or course substitutions:

> Since the early 1980s, the special education field has advocated for inclusion of special needs students in regular classes, including foreign language classes, with provisions for instructional and testing accommodations. These accommodations allow students with special needs to be successful in regular classes but mask their academic deficiencies, especially in language learning. More recently, though, special educators and disability advocates have recommended course substitutions and/or waivers for the foreign language requirement. As a consequence, there has been little or no interest in developing effective instructional methodologies for teaching foreign languages to students classified as LD and at-risk for language learning.[10]

I agree. So, in this book, I address that need by developing effective instructional methodologies specifically for at-risk students of foreign languages.

I often hear adults say that everyone can learn a second language because they have all learned their native language. That's certainly what I thought at the beginning of my career! But research and experience have shown me that while all people learn a native language, they nonetheless can have real difficulty learning another language—even if they begin in early schooling.

I've long wondered whether some languages might be easier or harder to learn than others, depending on students' particular language deficits. Is Spanish easier to learn than German? Than Japanese? I'll discuss some of these language-specific issues later in the book. For now, I'd like to point out that there are also common issues across languages—and potentially very similar ways of addressing them as teachers of at-risk learners. So although I teach French, I show how the same kinds of teaching-and-learning issues come up in languages like Spanish and German, and could arise even in English as a Second Language. In short, those of us who teach a second language to at-risk students can learn much from each other regardless of the specific languages we love and teach.

Certainly learning another language is hard work in and of itself, particularly for adults, who tend to be set in their cultural and linguistic ways. But I've learned that it's entirely possible to successfully teach struggling students another language. And it can be great fun too—for them and for you. After nearly four decades in the classroom, I'm a convert to teaching a second language to all students. I believe that all students should be given the opportunity to learn a foreign language. I also believe that, especially in a multicultural world, these students deserve teachers and materials that can help them through their individual difficulties.

Moreover, I contend that if current instructional approaches don't suit such students' learning needs, then our pedagogy needs to be adapted for them. Yes, we teachers are indeed part of the problem—not because we're cultural or academic elitists, but because we're just now learning how to teach such students wisely and well. I speak personally and passionately because I've developed such a method of instruction—one that is multisensory and highly structured, and includes a strong metacognitive component so that such students can become self-teaching. I've seen it work repeatedly to the joy and satisfaction of the students—and to my own delight as an educator, parent, and multicultural citizen. My approach includes direct and explicit instruction as well as many best practices. I invite you to witness the differences in students' lives—differences not just of students' better grades and completed courses, but of learners' self-esteem, self-confidence, and awareness of their own and others' cultures.

Your Invitation to New Ways of Teaching and Learning

This book explains my methodology with lots of concrete examples and illustrations. I invite you to learn how to teach more effectively, to laugh with me and my students, and to love yourself and your students. I hope that you'll join me and many other foreign-language instructors who have hearts for teaching at-risk students the joys of language and culture. I also hope that you'll join the expanding community of like-minded souls by visiting my website (www.foreignlanguagesforeveryone.com) and sharing ideas with colleagues throughout North America and increasingly around the world. Let's together contribute to the emerging cross-disciplinary conversations so we can all better serve our own students and colleagues. (Also on my website, you'll find all kinds of additional material that I didn't include in this book. I placed it on my website so I could update it regularly and provide it to you free of charge.) We're all important parts of the growing tapestry. Let's make it easier for our students to be both smart and productive. Thanks in advance to you for sharing your best practices and stories and questions with all of us seeking to serve such wonderful students.

In chapter 1, I look at multisensory aspects of such learning, including the auditory, visual, kinesthetic, and tactile dimensions. I discuss the importance of combining as many of the sensory channels as possible to embed learning. I provide specific, practical strategies in each of these areas.

I explain in chapter 2 the structured aspects of my approach, including classroom routine and environment, assignments, tests, presentation of content, handouts, and expectations of students. At-risk students generally appreciate structure. In second-language instruction, it's critically important if they are to flourish.

* see resource at www.foreignlanguagesforeveryone.com

In chapters 3 and 4, I discuss how metacognition—learning how we learn—can revolutionize our instruction. I first briefly summarize the research on metacognition so you understand what it is and why it's so important. Fear not—you can master metacognition, and so can your students. The tools are not complicated, but they are very effective. For instance, I explain how to employ a first-day questionnaire as well as student journals to help students better understand how they learn. Once at-risk learners really understand how they learn and which types of techniques will work for them, they are off and running with just some additional coaching along the way. In fact, they will begin helping you to teach them more effectively. The journals, in particular, will open your eyes, melt your heart, and inform your teaching.

I advocate in chapter 5 for direct and explicit instruction in phonology, morphology, and syntax. I additionally discuss the importance of relating foreign-language patterns back to English. I touch on the differences between inductive and deductive teaching, and then show various explicit strategies that help students learn. Learning how to teach directly and explicitly has revolutionized my success with at-risk students of all kinds.

In chapter 6, I suggest many best practices that you can use immediately. These include employing frequent repetition and review, attending to affective issues, facilitating cooperative learning, offering adjusted pacing and content, and varying the learning activities. Again, I provide lots of examples and illustrations, including stories of the humorous situations that arise when a teacher and student both seek excellence in teaching a second language to struggling learners. When we take ourselves as teachers a bit less seriously, our students quickly warm up to us and become less tense about their struggles and related anxieties. I even recommend having your students watch the episode of *I Love Lucy* in which dear Lucy directs her Cuban husband, Ricky, to begin reading books to their yet-unborn child in perfect English.*

In chapter 7, I discuss ways to help students take responsibility for their own learning. My suggestions include organizational skills, homework issues, testing, grading, and study aids. Regarding homework and testing, I elucidate unique ways of embedding learning: the IK Correction Method of correcting homework and tests, and the IK Grace Slip Method for discouraging late assignments without discouraging your students—yes, the "IK" is yours truly. I figured I should name something after myself because it's highly unlikely that anyone else will do so before I transition to the great foreign language in the world beyond! Seriously, these two methods take a bit more extra work outside the classroom, but you'll really appreciate the student responses.

Chapter 8 concludes the book with a discussion of what I've learned from my students, what they have learned about themselves, and what I recommend for further research.

My goal in this book is to integrate theory and praxis for the benefit of teachers and learners. My instructional approach has a strong theoretical basis. If you're interested, you can delve more deeply into that foundation by consulting the books, journal articles, and websites referenced throughout each chapter in the endnotes. I didn't fill chapters with all kinds of quotes from important researchers. I didn't want this book to read like academic work. So rather than using the in-text scientific notations that interfere with engaging reading, I used endnotes to cite research. I understand how busy we teachers are, and I know that we really appreciate educators who can help us understand and apply research. So that's what I've aimed to do in this book. But if you're working on a master's degree or you'd like to delve into the research on your own, please do read the endnotes and bibliography for tips and topics of interest. I've benefitted considerably from others' scholarly research. You will too.

I know firsthand how challenging it is to teach at-risk students a second language. I've lived in the same classrooms that you have—or that you will be dwelling in if you're new to the field—so I decided to quote frequently from my own students' journals. I chose not to put a "[*sic*]" by each error in the student journal excerpts or in the student responses to the first-day questionnaire because I wanted to preserve the flow and intent of their thoughts, as well as to maintain the dignity of the students who kindly gave me permission to use their entries in this book. Also, I've identified student journal entries in the book by putting them in italics.

I aim to inspire you to celebrate the joys of teaching at-risk students when you have the right ideas and tools in place. It's one thing to talk about what we teachers need to accomplish in a multicultural world with many struggling language learners. It's another thing to experience with our struggling students the joy of language and culture.

I humbly offer this book to foreign-language teachers and learning-disabilities specialists alike. I hope that all my foreign-language readers will learn that students who struggle can successfully learn another language and shouldn't be discouraged from doing so. I trust that my readers in the learning disabilities field will discover in this book ideas that will be especially helpful for students who are required to demonstrate some level of foreign-language mastery. I don't expect my foreign-language colleagues who read this book to totally revamp their existing successful programs, but I hope that you'll discover some new ideas that will integrate effectively with your own, developing methods. You might be the next one to write a paper, journal article, or book that helps all of us learn how to better serve our at-risk learners.

Along the way, I sincerely desire that you become even more aware of both the struggles of at-risk students and their incredible potential for serving our increasingly diverse communities around the globe. I know that by studying how we can enhance at-risk students' language acquisition, we are also discovering ways of enhancing foreign-language instruction for learners of all kinds. The theories, methods, and best practices that help at-risk learners can benefit all learners.

A Few Words about Terms and People

During the years that I worked on this book, the term "foreign language" was gradually being replaced by the term "world language." I decided to stick with the former phrase in this book for several reasons. First, I used the term for many years and am comfortable with it. Second, I prefer the term because I think it is more accurate than "world language"—which in common English usage suggests a global or worldwide language. Third, the largest international language teachers' association in the world—the American Council on the Teaching of Foreign Languages (ACTFL)*—still uses my preferred term. Finally, most research literature uses it. I aimed with this and other terms to maintain consistency for people doing keyword searches in databases and online.

Also, I have tried to use terms such as "learning disabled" or "attention-deficit hyperactivity disorder" (ADHD) very carefully and sensitively. I have intentionally used these terms, but in the sense of describing at-risk or struggling students as "students with learning disabilities" rather than "learning-disabled students." A person's disability does not ultimately define who that person is, any more than someone's marital status, profession, or gender. These are simply aspects of the totality of a human being. Thus a person "*has* ADHD," not "*is* ADHD."

Finally, I decided not to use in this book many of the common educational acronyms such as LD (learning disabilities), L2 (second language), and TL (target language). I suspect that some readers will be part-time and volunteer instructors who are not as familiar with such acronyms, so I decided to be as linguistically hospitable to them as possible. On the other hand, an acronym such as ADHD is so widely known and used beyond educational circles that I have used it and a few other linguistic shortcuts.

Discovering Delight in Teaching Struggling Second-Language Learners

To conclude this introductory chapter, I'd like to cite a moving journal entry from one of my students who had switched from the nursing program (with no foreign-language requirement) to a regular BA degree program with a foreign-language requirement:

> *I just wanted to write about how much I appreciate the different ways of learning this class is taught in. . . . For someone like me who, up until a year ago, hated learning more than anything, hated school, hated anything that had to do with it, because it was hard, because it was frustrating, because it was defeating; this class has truly been a blessing for me. As much as I may complain about repetition, or act like I am not paying attention in class, or that I could not care any less, that is not the case. For me, learning comes at a price, and usually that price is my emotions, my self-esteem, and frustration, but after being diagnosed with ADHD* [attention-deficit hyperactivity disorder] *and starting medication and then shortly afterwards enrolling in French . . . ,* [I've learned] *so much. It has given me an alternative way to learn and a reason to enjoy education. It has given me a reason to think that I have the possibility to learn this well in all of my classes and throughout life. So thanks a lot!*

Isn't this why you entered teaching? Isn't it why we educators learn new methods—to better serve our students? This student's painful journey should motivate us to reexamine our own teaching. Learning should never come at an unnecessarily negative emotional price for students. The problems we face teaching foreign languages to challenged students are opportunities for us to learn and grow with them. When I read a journal entry like this one, I give thanks for such students. Their determination is inspiring. Their accomplishments are so satisfying to them, their families, and their teachers. To witness firsthand such students' life growth is among the most gratifying experiences in my life. Little did I know many decades ago that memories of my father's inverted queries on the telephone would come back to me as I began the journey of teaching at-risk students the joy of learning a second language and dwelling in a new culture.

1

Engaging Students in Multisensory Ways

I recently retook a training class for using an automated external defi-brillator (AED). We were encouraged to locate the unit nearest our offices and touch the box. It was solid instructional advice. Why? Because it engaged our multiple senses as a way of embedding the location in our brains.

Consider this: could you quickly identify the letter *f* on your keyboard without putting your hands on the keyboard in QWERTY formation?[1] Or this: would you more readily remember a person's name by hearing it, seeing it, or simultaneously hearing and seeing it?

These are important matters for hands-on learners. I'll address them in this chapter on multisensory teaching and learning. We'll first take a brief look at the research literature and then at how the visual, auditory, and kinesthetic/tactile modes can be used in a foreign-language class. We'll also briefly explore the olfactory mode. I believe that multisensory teaching is beneficial for all students—not just for at-risk students—because it engages the whole person.

Much has been written about multisensory teaching, both for native-language and foreign-language learning. From the earliest days of the Orton-Gillingham method for teaching students to read in English, to more recent approaches for teaching at-risk students, ample evidence demonstrates the effectiveness of incorporating multisensory practices into the classroom.[2] For a deeper examination of the research literature, remember to consult the sources in this book and on my website.[3]

As I examine the various sensory modes, you'll notice that they often overlap. Sometimes one mode is primary; at other times, I suggest using several modes simultaneously. While I don't employ every mode daily, I'm constantly experimenting in order to discover new ways to use the various senses to better embed learning. I aim to reach all students in their own sensory uniqueness.

Listening to the Auditory Mode

I once worked with the French CEO of a local company who wanted to improve his English. He often pronounced English sounds in a distinctly French way (e.g., he pronounced "rubber nipples" as "rubber neeples"). The English word "forsythia" was almost impossible for him to reproduce, until I broke the word down into its constituent parts and pronounced each syllable for him, showing him where I placed my tongue—behind my teeth or between them. As long as he didn't *hear* the individual sounds, he simply couldn't reproduce the word with the *s* and *th* sounds in the right place. Likewise, students must be able to *hear* new sounds in order to produce them correctly. Tricky words and sounds that don't exist in English (e.g., French or German *r* and *u* sounds, or the Spanish *r* sound), must be examined especially closely. Students need to learn which part of the mouth, throat, and nose to use for these sounds. In the classroom and in work with tutors, my students focus carefully on learning all the different sounds of French, and I provide detailed handouts* for vowels and consonants. All languages have particular sounds that need to be carefully demonstrated by the teacher and learned by the students.

In a typical foreign-language classroom, the most frequently used sensory mode is auditory. For many of my students, this mode is very weak, because their auditory processing is very slow, their auditory memory is poor, or they have difficulty hearing sound distinctions. For them, the visual or kinesthetic mode is much stronger. These students need help developing strategies to strengthen their auditory skills. For example, I help students carefully break down new words and phrases into discernible sound segments.

Even though I grew up in a bilingual home (Dutch and English), I remember marveling at how our Italian neighbors could understand

* see resource at www.foreignlanguagesforeveryone.com

each other while talking so fast—and sometimes even with food in their mouths! When you hear people speaking to each other in a language you don't know, can you tell where words begin and end? At-risk students have a hard time breaking down the speech stream into recognizable sounds and words. To them, a foreign language is like one long river of sounds that all run together. My students need lots of listening practice in homework assignments and in class.

Each of my chapter tests has a listening section (usually a dialog) with questions to be answered in English. I give students time to look over the questions so they can anticipate what they're listening for. I conduct each listening portion of the test twice. Students first listen to the script in its entirety, trying to answer as many questions as possible. Then I briefly stop the dialog at the specific spots where the answers to specific questions are located. Pausing the speech stream gives students time to mull over the last few words they heard and to try to make sense out of them. If the recording is somewhat unclear, or if a lot of students look stymied, I will sometimes repeat the salient phrase. Students try desperately to separate the sound segments and put them back together into something intelligible; by momentarily stopping the recording, I give students a second chance to understand sentences that otherwise would likely be incomprehensible.

Many students with weak auditory processing simply don't hear cognates in the target language. A cognate is written but not necessarily pronounced the same in the target language as in English. The French word *multiplication*, for instance, is spelled exactly the same in English.* But when spoken aloud to a weak auditory learner, the word doesn't instantiate the English word *multiplication*, because the vowel and consonant sounds are quite different and the stress falls on a different syllable (in French, on the last syllable). If those same students saw the word written out, however, they would immediately recognize it as a cognate.

I regularly use music* and singing*—even though my students are generally not good singers. There is a growing body of research on music and the brain, especially with the recent innovations in brain-imaging scans. For instance, studies have examined the transfer effect of musical training on cognitive functions, including language, as well as the connection between dyslexia and rhythm.[4]

I believe that music embeds learning by bypassing rational cognition. Why is it that people with Alzheimer's disease, who are no longer able to speak, can still sing the songs of their youth? Oliver Sacks says all people seem to respond to music, especially senior citizens and patients suffering from a stroke or dementia, suggesting that this impact must be a result of something within basic brain structure. He writes, "This most universal responsiveness to music is an essential part of our neural nature. Though analogies often are made to birdsong or animal cries, music in its full sense . . . seems to be confined to our own species, like language. Why this should be so is still a mystery. Our research is only now beginning to unlock those secrets."[5]

One example of musical learning in my classroom is teaching students the well-known children's alphabet song; we sing it in the target language, with some slight adjustments.[6] When students wonder what a given letter of the alphabet is, they can simply hum the song in their heads in order to recall the correct letter sound. Another helpful children's song with kinesthetic elements is "Head and Shoulders, Knees and Toes," which I translated into French. It's as squeeze to fit in all the words, but the students gladly get up out of their seats and sing* enthusiastically "*Tête, épaules, genoux et pieds, genoux et pieds!*" while pointing to their heads, shoulders, knees, and feet. Those who teach other languages could do similar things.

I've also discovered that forming a kind of Gregorian chant out of a basic grammar rule works well for embedding learning. An example of this is what I call the *pas de* rule in French, which stipulates that the indefinite articles *un, une, des* ("a/an, some") become *de* ("any") in a negative sentence. This is the equivalent in English of changing the affirmative sentence "I have a pencil" to "I have no pencil" or to "I don't have a pencil," or literally "I have not any pencil." I want my students to remember this concept, so I created a chant* that goes as follows:

> ♫ ♪ *Pas de, pas de, pas de,*
> *Un, une, des* become *de* after *pas!* ♫ ♪

I explain to students that this rule functions like a sort of "autocorrect" on the computer.

Looking at the Visual Mode

One of the most frustrating interpersonal dynamics is being introduced to someone and almost immediately forgetting their name. The next time

* see resource at www.foreignlanguagesforeveryone.com

we meet, we're usually too embarrassed to ask for the name. Most of us are more likely to remember a person's name if we also see it on a name tag. We struggle to remember things that we only hear, more than we do to recall things that we see as well. This is a common phenomenon for most people, but it's especially true for students with poor auditory processing.

So a significant instructional challenge is making highly auditory foreign-language teaching more visual. I do this in a variety of ways:

1. Overhead transparencies
2. Daily gray sheets
3. Color-coded handouts
4. Daily repetition of vocabulary
5. Highlighting pens

Let's take a closer look at each of these visual approaches.

Using Overhead Transparencies

Rather than presenting grammar concepts and culture purely verbally, I make these concepts visual during class by writing on overhead transparencies the basic information for the day's lessons. I make transparencies from PowerPoint slides so I can underline, circle endings, and fill in blanks right on the transparencies during class. I encourage students to do the same on the paper copies I give them. These transparencies serve as the outline from which I teach. I generally avoid using a blackboard or a whiteboard at the front of the classroom because they require me to turn my back on students, thereby losing my own visual connection with them. By writing on a transparency during class, I can continue to look at my students and confirm whether they're comprehending, staying engaged, and following along on their copies. This is crucial in a classroom where many students have attention issues; they easily lose focus due to their inability to attend at length to a new concept being taught. Writing on a blackboard is also ephemeral—the content is in front of the students one moment, and erased the next.

Employing Daily Gray Sheets

Students who have problems with visual-motor integration and written expression learn better when they receive copies of notes rather than having to copy a lot of material from a blackboard, overhead projection, or PowerPoint presentation. So I give my students a copy of the overhead transparencies on a "daily gray sheet"(see supplement 1)* with four over-heads per page.[7] Students can follow along as I explain new concepts rather than worrying about correctly writing down all the notes.

For many at-risk students, it's difficult to follow along and pay attention while simultaneously taking notes accurately in class. That's why so many students with documented learning disabilities are accorded the fairly standard accommodation of being allowed a note taker. None of my students have ever asked for this accommodation because they all get the daily gray handout.

The handout provides students with an overview of each day's lesson and serves as a visual organizer, telling students what is important. This is particularly helpful for students with attention-deficit hyperactivity disorder (ADHD), who can have a hard time sifting out the most salient parts of a lesson. In addition to listing new grammatical or cultural concepts, the handout includes that day's vocabulary quiz and any songs or meditations for that day.

I also alert students when I am going to express a key point in a lesson. I do this by encouraging students to add notes and marking—such as a circle, asterisk, or underscore—while they're following along. Many students with attention difficulties need help knowing where to focus their attention.

Because the main points of the lesson are already written down, some students might tune out. To avoid this problem, I purposely leave blanks here and there so that students need to stay focused and fill in the missing pieces as we go through each overhead transparency. Occasionally students have said that they find it more helpful to write out the notes themselves, rather than use the gray sheet. They can always do that while still using the handout as a backup.

In their journals, students discuss how helpful the daily gray sheet is to them. One wrote, "*I think that the gray sheets are the biggest help for me. When I took Spanish, my notes would always be missing things or I just wouldn't understand them but the sheets work out well for reference and studying.*" Another student journaled, "*I really appreciate all the visual work that you do on the overhead and that you have us do. To simply listen to the French language would be impossible for me to understand so thank you for being aware of visual learners.*" Yet another one remarked, "*I really like that we get the handouts of all of the overheads so that we can*

* see resource at www.foreignlanguagesforeveryone.com

focus more on what is being talked about in class and not worrying about whether or not we wrote everything down." Many at-risk students are poor spellers. If they were copying notes, they would invariably misspell words and omit things. Students truly need correct spelling in language learning. When learning new verb endings, for example, if they inadvertently reverse two letters and then study from those notes, they will end up spending their precious learning time memorizing the wrong endings. Having it written correctly on an overhead and on the gray sheet allows them to focus on the form, to detect patterns, and to add things that will help them remember the new information.

Color-Coding Handouts

Another aspect of my multisensory approach is color-coded and even paper-coded handouts.[8] In my classes, when students see the color of a handout, they immediately know what kind of material it is and where it has to go in their notebooks. Students also recognize that something printed on card stock rather than regular copy paper must be especially important. This is a tremendous help for at-risk students who have difficulty with organization due to their deficits in sequential ordering and spatial organization—what Mel Levine calls "material management dysfunction."[9] My students must use a binder with tab inserts for all color-coded and card stock class handouts. I love the "music" of students' binders clicking open and shut, because I know that their materials are going directly into the right place and can be accessed quickly when needed. Disorganized students are sometimes amazed by their ability to organize materials using this system, so they use it in other classes as well.

Seeing and Repeating Daily Vocabulary Words

Anyone who has taken music lessons remembers endlessly rehearsing basic scales. The repetition can be torturous, but it strengthens hands and fingers while mentally linking finger movements to musical notes on a page. Like the keys on a piano or the holes in a flute, words are the building blocks of language and must be learned to the point of becoming automatic. I give students a daily vocabulary quiz to ensure that they're working on mastering the tools they need to produce language as fluently as possible.

Students need to learn not only the meaning and spelling of words but also the correct pronunciation, which I spend much time reviewing. Before each quiz, students get out their pink vocabulary sheets and carefully look at each word and phrase while simultaneously repeating them after me. This allows the students to use three sensory modes for embedding the words: seeing, hearing, and saying. We go over the words and phrases for the next day's quiz before reviewing the vocabulary for the current day's quiz, so that these are fresh in the students' minds.

As part of their daily homework, students prepare for each day's quiz partly by listening to recordings of pronounced words. The files are in a downloadable format so students can listen to them online or on their own portable players. While I record the words myself, many textbook publishers now include such recordings.

Using Highlighters

Because in many languages nouns are gendered, it's important that students learn the correct gender with each word.* The gender of words isn't always logical, and because English has no gender, this can be a relatively tricky concept to master. If students don't learn the correct gender from the start, they'll have difficulty later with adjective and verb agreement. So I encourage my students to use pink (for feminine) and blue (for masculine) highlighters to color code the nouns on their vocabulary sheets. This provides an extra visual marker for learning genders. A third color can be added for languages such as German and Latin, which also have the neuter gender.[10]

Touching Students with Kinesthetic Modes

Some time ago I needed physical therapy. After each session, the therapist would give me a sheet of paper with pictures and words explaining the new activity that I was to incorporate into my daily regimen. While the sheet was helpful when I got home, what had been the most helpful to me was the actual doing of the exercise—putting my body through the motions. The therapist always had me practice the motion a few times before sending me home to do the therapy. I learned quickly that if I could *feel* what I had to do—as well as hear it, read about it, and see a picture of it—I was much more likely to remember how to do the routine.

This is an example of how the kinesthetic mode can help embed learning. Doing therapy at home also required counting the number of repetitions performed (e.g., five repetitions of holding a position to a count of ten). I

* see resource at www.foreignlanguagesforeveryone.com

found that if I said aloud the number at the start of each set, I was much more likely to be able to keep track of where I was in the routine than if I simply said the number in my head. If I added a tactile component—if I held up my fingers to represent the number of repetitions—I'd be even more likely to remember it, because this information was now reaching my brain via the extremely strong tactile mode of learning.

I remember the struggles my younger daughter had with memorizing her weekly Bible verses for school. What ended up working well for her was putting the verses to a kind of rap/rhythm, and adding hand gestures where appropriate. One verse that will forever stick in her (and my!) memory is the phrase "and set him high upon a rock." She remembered that part by hitting the fist of one hand into the open palm of the other hand when she got to the word "rock." If we incorporate body gestures into our teaching, we will greatly help many students.[11]

Howard Gardner, one of the pioneers in the study of the different ways that people learn, says "bodily-kinesthetic" intelligence involves "the potential of using one's whole body or parts of the body (like the hand or the mouth) to solve problems or fashion products."[12] This form of intelligence is often very strong among at-risk learners, so I try to incorporate many such activities into my teaching. They often can't be categorized as purely tactile or purely kinesthetic because they frequently include additional sensory components (e.g., visual or auditory). Below I've divided them into kinesthetic and tactile according to their primary characteristics, using French as the sample target language.

There are many different whole-body activities a creative teacher could incorporate into foreign-language teaching. Here are some that I have developed and found quite helpful for at-risk students. Although I use them for teaching French, they are easily adaptable for other languages.

1. Using wide rubber bands to teach syllabification and stress
2. Tapping out syllables
3. Raising an arm for intonation patterns or accents
4. Clapping hands to embed numbers

Stretching Wide Rubber Bands

The short, wide, strong elastic bands that come on stalks of vegetables can be used to teach syllabification and stress within words and phrases.

Students and I hold the rubber band between our thumbs. I then slowly say a multisyllabic word, gently pulling out on each syllable, and giving a strong pull on the syllable where the stress falls. The students repeat the word, pulling gently for each syllable, and then pulling strongly on the stressed syllable. For example, I have students repeat the phrase *une - cal-cu-la-TRICE* ("a calculator"), giving a strong pull on the final syllable. Once they have done this, I jokingly remark, "It's importANT to put the emPHAsis on the right sylLAble!" Students immediately catch on. We do several more iterations of the same phrase and then different phrases such as *Fé-li-ci-ta-TIONS* ("Congratulations"); *un - a-é-ro-PORT* ("an airport"); *une - bou-lan-ge-RIE* ("a bakery"). This enables the students to hear the syllabification, see it written out, say it, and feel it in their hands. When we use these four modes, the concept of syllabification and stress can enter the brain via multiple sensory modes. The same thing can be done with progressively longer phrases or entire sentences.

Tapping Out Syllables

A similar activity can be done by having students tap out syllables on their desk. I demonstrate each word or phrase, tapping lightly for each syllable and then giving a strong, sustained tap at the end of the word or phrase, where the stress falls.

Raising an Arm for Intonation Patterns or Accents

People often admire the French language's beautiful sounds, which are due largely to the rising and falling intonation patterns that render it music-like.[13] These patterns can be demonstrated by doing an upward or downward motion of the arm and allowing students to feel whether the intonation of each segment is rising or falling.

In many languages, accent marks affect the pronunciation of a word. At-risk students often find them confusing and difficult to master. When teaching accent marks, I sometimes have students raise their arms in a sweeping motion to get a feel for whether an accent mark goes up or down. It sometimes seems rather hokey to students, but they really remember the concept after their brains have received it kinesthetically.

Clapping Hands to Embed Numbers

For reviewing low numbers (one to twenty), I've devised a kinesthetic activity called *Concentration*. It's a variation of the similarly named English game, which I translated into French. Ideally students are seated in a circle or semicircle. I give each student a number from one to X (X = the number of students in the class); the teacher can also play, taking either the lowest (when students are still learning the game) or the last number. Assign numbers in the order of the seats in the circle, or have students randomly draw numbers from a bag. The students must seat themselves in numerical order. Going around the room, students say their number aloud in ascending order in the target language so that they get review practice. The entire group begins the game by singing rhythmically. While they're singing, they're also clapping their hands twice in the air and then hitting their desk twice with their palms down. The song goes like this:

♫ ♪ '*Con-cen-tra-tion! Con-cen-tra-tion! Prêts, com-mence!*' ♫ ♪ {Concentration! (clap, clap, hit, hit) Concentration! Ready, begin! (clap, clap, hit, hit)}

At that point, the person who is number one (with everyone continuing to clap twice and hit twice) shouts in the target language, "One, one (clap, clap), four, four (hit, hit)." Student four, keeping the rhythm, then has to say, "Four, four (clap, clap), two, two (hit, hit)." Next, student two keeps the rhythm going and the game continues until a student errs. Then that student goes to the end of the line, taking the number of the last person, and everyone upstream from that student moves up one slot and assumes a new lower number. If student three makes an error, students one and two don't move, but everyone else does. All the numbers are repeated aloud around the circle so that everyone knows their new numbers. Finally, play resumes. The goal of the game is to get to the number one slot and stay there.

This game can be played for five minutes or longer. It's a good activity to save for the end of class, especially as a closing activity, or if there is some time left over at the end of class. Students report that doing this kinesthetic/tactile activity really helps them learn numbers. Interestingly, some students are unable to clap and focus on the numbers at the same time. They get totally out of sync with the rhythm, or don't even clap, apparently because their entire attention has to remain focused on the numbers being called out.

Although it might at first be a bit embarrassing for some students to participate in this kind of game, I've never had a student who refused to participate. It's fine if they don't clap, but if their number gets called, they are expected to play along by saying their own number twice and then someone else's number in order to keep the game going. Mostly we laugh a lot during this game. A few students write in their journals that this is one of their least favorite class activities. The game never lasts too long—about five minutes at the end of class. I think if I gave the option not to participate in a given classroom activity, given my population of students, there would be quite a few who would ask not to have to do an oral presentation (due to extremely high anxiety), but I think very few would ask not to play *Concentration*.

You could devise other clapping activities for language practice. For example, some students remember childhood games in which they clapped hands with a partner and sang little songs. These could easily be made into a rhythmic clapping activity to practice the conjugation of important verbs, for example.

Tactile Activities

The range of possible tactile activities* is vast. Some of those I describe below are my own creations. Others are variations of what many wonderful teachers do (for example, tossing a beach ball rather than a soft ball). I think the activities could all be used in any language. Please share with me any ideas you have here and I will be happy to add them to the list on my website.*

1. Writing on whiteboards
2. Tossing a soft ball
3. Handling "fiddle gadgets"
4. Writing out or tracing over difficult words
5. Bumping fists together for elision

6. Doing hands-on vocabulary activities

Writing on Whiteboards

One of the most important tactile components I use regularly is whiteboards. They're primarily tactile because students write out words or draw pictures on them. They help a student hear, write, and say a concept. Such boards are good for reviewing material, but they can also work for leading students inductively into a new concept—such as having the students predict and write out how a verb in the present perfect tense might look if it were conjugated with "to be" rather than with "to have." Whiteboards even give fidgety students something tactile to focus on.

Some at-risk students find whiteboards so essential to their learning that they ask to borrow one for the entire year. For instance, they say that when they conjugate a verb on one, the resulting dark ink on the white background helps them remember its forms. One student wrote, *"I like using the* [white] *boards. . . . They're fun but also they waste less paper and I like that I can write big with different colors because then I can picture them better in my head."* Another student recalled, *"The use of whiteboards was crucial to my success, and I really needed to write the new grammar rules out as I was learning them."* Sometimes I ask students to trade colors of pens for adding prefixes or endings to verbs—something that makes these language elements stand out more clearly.

Whiteboards can also be used to quickly review irregular verbs. I divide the class into two teams and give each one a board, a marker, and an eraser. The first person writes the infinitive and its meaning at the top; the board is then passed on from student to student until all the subject pronouns and corresponding verb forms are written correctly. Students are encouraged to correct any errors they see. Group collaboration leads them to discuss together what the right form is, allowing them to learn from each other. Once the team is done, they hold up the board for my review. Meanwhile, the other team keeps working, since it's possible the winning team has erred. If there is an error, I tell the team that there's *un petit problème* ("a little problem") and give them a chance to correct it. If it's correct, I wait until the other team is done and has it right before declaring a winner—to keep all the students on task as long as possible.

The first team to get the entire verb written correctly wins, but I wait until both teams are done, look to make sure both are correct, and then hold up both boards for the students to verbally repeat the correct forms. I then declare a win. Students enjoy this activity partly because it enables them to review verbs in a manner that is collaborative and somewhat competitive, and uses the tactile and kinesthetic modes.

Using highly competitive games with at-risk students isn't always a good idea. Some students thrive on such activities because it fits their ability to work well under pressure—like some students with ADHD who need a deadline in order to perform well. But other students greatly dislike competitive games, probably partly because they have vividly painful memories of prior experiences where they were picked last when teams were chosen and neither team wanted them. I recommend making strongly competitive activities more collaborative.

Sometimes I individualize the activity by giving students their own board, pen, and eraser. I encourage them to compare what they have written with what their neighbor has written and discuss or defend their choice. I might have students practice a new verb tense with the different subject pronouns. I give each phrase in English, and the students write them in French. I say, for example, "I will arrive," and the students need to write *j'arriverai*. As the students write out their forms, I uncover the correct answers, one at a time, on an overhead transparency, so that students can check whether they wrote the phrase correctly. We then repeat it together aloud. By making an overhead for each group of verb forms (which will then be part of the daily gray sheet), I provide students with a visual document to review on their own.

Tossing a Soft Ball

Another useful tactile tool is a soft toy—such as a sponge ball or a small stuffed toy—that can be readily caught with one hand. This is used to quickly review the four "big verbs" in French: *être* ("to be"), *avoir* ("to have"), *aller* ("to go"), and *faire* ("to make; to do"). Because these verbs need constant review, I employ this activity frequently. I state the infinitive form of the verb and throw the ball to a random student, who then gives the "I" form in the target language. This student then throws the ball to another student, who must give the "you" (familiar) form. That student then throws it to yet another student, and play continues until all of the forms are correctly given. Some basic ground rules need to be established: students are to throw the ball gently, and all students must be ready to catch it at any time. This activity works best when students are seated in a semicircle.

A colleague varies this activity by having students stand in a circle and conjugate verbs while tossing a beach ball. Various wedges of the ball have different colors that correspond to different pronouns. A student who catches the ball then has to conjugate a sentence using the pronoun represented by the colored wedge being touched by most of the student's right hand.[14] While the students toss the ball, the teacher randomly switches the verb, so that students get practice with different forms of different verbs. This teacher also employs a dice game for which paired students receive two dice. The first die represents the six subject pronouns; the second die represents any six verbs that the instructor wants the students to work on that day. Depending on the proficiency level of the students, the instructor has them work together as a group, take turns, or race to conjugate the verb the most quickly.

For example, the student rolls the two dice and the first die lands on "to speak" and the second on "we." The student would then be expected to say "we speak" correctly in the target language. This could be done in pairs where students would simply be working together, going back and forth, to conjugate different verbs. If it were a race, one person would roll the dice (maybe the teacher?), and the first person of each team would have to correctly say or write "we speak." Whoever did so correctly first would get a point for that team. The dice would be rolled again, and the second person in each team would play for the point. Play would continue until all the team members had had a turn. Another less competitive version would be to have the teams work together to come up with the correct form and present it to the teacher (probably writing it on a whiteboard) to earn a point for their team.

Handling "Fiddle Gadgets"

Many students love fiddling with something during learning. If you give them markers for drawing, they're suddenly stacking them end to end or tapping their desks with them. Some of my students with ADHD have recurring difficulty sitting still and staying focused on classroom activities. So I always take several different fiddle gadgets* to class. These seem to work well, especially during longer class sessions.[15]

One such gadget is "fiddlesticks"—movable, brightly colored wooden blocks that have an elastic string running through them, allowing students to twist them into different shapes. Another gadget is a stress ball—a rubber ball filled with a kind of putty that holds its shape for short periods of time. Heavy latex balloons can be filled with sand and used similarly. All such manipulable items can help particular students focus on what's going on in the classroom. Some teachers give their students Silly Putty or Play-Doh. The latter could also be used for vocabulary development, having students (especially in elementary school) form different fruits, for example, to show that they know the meaning of the words. Simply having something in their hands seems to help many of them focus. I find that many students pay closer attention when they have something to do with their hands. Many students find it helpful to doodle on a piece of paper, for example.*

I don't allow students to use their laptops or other distracting devices to "fiddle." On the few occasions when students have asked me if they could use their laptops to take notes, I simply reminded them that the daily gray sheets are perfect for taking organized, accurate notes. Students have always been satisfied with that answer.

I've read about classrooms where students are allowed to sit on large balancing balls as a way to remain engaged. Perhaps some students would do well standing up by a high table at the back of the classroom.

Writing Out or Tracing Over Difficult Words

The tactile mode can also be used to help with difficult spellings. At-risk students frequently reverse vowels in words. The word for "yesterday" (*hier*) is likely to be spelled incorrectly as *heir*. Students can use their fingers in a number of ways to embed the correct spelling. Many find it helpful to write out difficult words ten times; I often see them doing this right before the daily vocabulary quiz. Not surprisingly, these students consistently have the highest quiz grades. I sometimes suggest this method if a student has misspelled the same word several times on a homework assignment—in order to employ the tactile mode to embed the word correctly into the brain.

* see resource at www.foreignlanguagesforeveryone.com

I also suggest that students write a troublesome word in large printed letters on a full sheet of paper. Then they can use their nondominant hand to trace over each letter with their index finger, while simultaneously saying, seeing, and feeling each letter. I suggest their nondominant hand because I theorize that this activity stimulates another pathway to the brain. Young children might have at home a small sandbox in which they could write the difficult words in the sand with the index finger of their nondominant hand. In some languages, words don't follow predictable sound/symbol patterns; students might better learn these nonphonetic words by tracing or writing the letters of the word while saying the letter name rather than its sound.[16]

Bumping Fists Together for Elision

I devised a two-handed gesture of bumping fists into each other as a way to help students remember French's elision rule, which says that two vowels can't stand next to ("bump") each other in particular contexts. I use this gesture regularly in class as a tactile memory tool. An example of this is the use of *le* or *la* ("the") before a word that begins with a vowel sound. Both of those words will become *l'* instead. Hence, *le oeuf* ("the egg") becomes *l'oeuf* and *la église* ("the church") becomes *l'église*. Other languages have similar patterns for which the tactile mode could be employed.

Doing Hands-On Vocabulary Activities

For vocabulary development, I often bring real-life objects to class so that students can touch them. With a unit on school supplies, for example, I bring a backpack with a pencil, paper, book, eraser, calculator, notebook, and the like. I ask students to review the items as I pull them out of a backpack. You can also do this with categories such as toiletries (e.g., shampoo, toilet paper, comb, toothpaste, toothbrush), plastic fruits and vegetables, other foods, and clothing. For a unit on body parts, pairs of students can use male and female dolls. One partner asks in the target language, "What is this?" The other partner answers, "This is the (head)." For a unit on clothing, I bring a bag of culturally authentic clothing, such as a French *béret*, and hold up one item at a time, asking the students to identify each one. I then pass each item around the room, telling the first student the name of the item, including the article to reinforce each word's gender. The first student passes it to the next student, repeating the phrase. Each item goes around the room until the last person hands it back to me, repeating the item's name and article.

Sensing Olfactory Modes

When I was little, my mother carried a bottle of No. 4711 eau de cologne in her purse. She would sometimes put a few drops of it on her lace hand-kerchief during church or when she was feeling light-headed. More than two decades after her passing, I still remember her whenever I smell that cologne. Most people have childhood memories strongly connected with specific smells—such as the aroma of frying bacon connected to Saturday-morning breakfasts or camping trips. Smell is one of the strongest sensory modes, but we don't really know much about its instructional use.

I haven't figured out yet how to incorporate it into my teaching. There is a strong emotive component to olfaction, enabling people to remember something from the distant past simply by smelling something from that time.[17] Researchers have determined that the sense of smell diminishes with age and some forms of dementia.[18] Other research examines the role of olfaction in memorizing word lists. Children given olfactory informa-tion along with a word list recall words more easily and retain them more effectively than children given the lists without olfactory cues.[19] It would be wonderful to be able to help students' memories by tapping into the olfactory sense—or perhaps even to help them create new memories related to their use of a second language. This area warrants further research for foreign-language learning.

The Value of Multisensory Teaching

Multisensory teaching is vitally important for students who struggle with foreign-language learning. We rightly think of language as speech and assume that it is primarily auditory. But of course we all use language in the midst of our other senses as well. We learn a first language by seeing, hearing, smelling, touching, and the like. So it shouldn't surprise us that students might learn a new language more quickly, fully, or memorably when teachers use as many senses as possible. I am convinced that audi-tory learning is weak for many at-risk students. By adding the visual, kinesthetic, and tactile modes, we can enhance learning. I'm grateful that even someone teaching a professor how to use an automated external defibrillator recognized this fact.

2

Providing Parameters for Student Success

A student arrives for class with a great attitude—seemingly eager to learn, smiling warmly, happily chatting with friends. But he's also a few minutes late, entering the room noisily with fanfare. He can't find his pencil, so he borrows one from a friend. Then he starts rummaging dramatically through all of the junk in his backpack in hopes of finding his homework—much to the delight of onlookers. From somewhere in the bowels of his messy backpack, he finally digs out his completed assignment, albeit crumpled, a little dog-eared, and colored with mustard.

If this is common, the student probably has issues that will impede learning in a foreign-language classroom. How can this student be helped to succeed? Among other things, this kind of student is more likely to flourish in a structured environment that provides needed boundaries.

In this chapter, I describe what I've learned about structured aspects of the foreign-language pedagogy. Scholars typically use the term "structured" rather generically in conjunction with the term "multisensory."[1] I will explain what I mean by structure and how I employ it in my own teaching. As I developed my teaching approach, I began to use the word "structure" to refer to students with various organizational and attention issues. Such students—who have difficulty with organization or focus—need an overall structured learning framework so they understand how teachers approach (1) classroom environment, (2) learning routine, (3) assignments,*

(4) tests, (5) presentation of content, (6) handouts, and (7) the expectations of students. Let's take a closer look at each of these now.

Creating a Classroom Environment

What kind of classroom environments did you experience as a student—chairs in a circle, desks in rigid rows? Were there classrooms where you felt welcome and supported in your learning, or classrooms where you didn't? What were those classrooms like? I think that teachers in my day generally took such things for granted. When it comes to teaching at-risk learners, however, the classroom environment needs to be considered as part of structured teaching and learning.

Classroom Setup

I want to briefly stress the importance of a physically structured classroom environment.* The first few years I taught the modified sequence, I met in a small seminar room with students who sat in chairs around a large table. That was a relaxed and friendly environment, but some students felt they didn't have enough room to spread out their binders and books, and a few students found it difficult to sit so close to others because it seemed to violate their personal space—and made it too easy to see each other's work. Eventually we switched to a more traditional classroom with desks in rows. I don't like teaching to rows because I can't easily see all students to make sure I'm connecting with them as I teach. Also, rows don't seem to promote active learning.

I learned to situate desks in a semicircle, two or three desks deep, so that all the students can see me and each other. This layout allows me to circulate among them easily when they're doing paired activities. It also provides a natural environment for speaking activities. Since language learning is very interactive, the classroom must encourage natural person-to-person exchange. Shortly after I first made the switch to semicircles, one student journaled with numerous spelling and other errors, *"My thoughts on the know environment is that I like the class it is nice there is a little more space. I do like the old room as well though it was nice to be around a table. I like the class room because there is a bigger chalk board. I like the class because it is less stuffy. I like the other room because it seems a little cozier; it reminds me of being around my table at home doing homework."* Another student wrote that when desks aren't in rows, it creates a *"community approach."*

* see resource at www.foreignlanguagesforeveryone.com

The student added, "*You were able to get to know people in the class better and it made class not so painful to go to.*"

Outdoor Distractions

Students with attention issues can be easily distracted, so I always close window coverings and shut the door. I aim to reduce extraneous noise. I work hard to minimize any external distractions, such as voices in the hallway. On a sunny February day in Michigan, I mercifully leave the curtains open on the edges to let in a little sun, but not open enough to divert students' attention to outdoor activities.

Establishing a Learning Routine

Can you recall some of the classroom routines that teachers used when you were a student? Did some of your teachers establish a very orderly classroom and a set routine so that you knew exactly what to expect when you entered their classroom? Did you have other teachers whose daily routines were less formally structured—maybe even a bit chaotic? Did you know from one day to the next what those classes would bring? Did you personally learn better in the highly structured or less-structured situations?

Most students probably learn well from both kinds of instructors. At-risk students, however, learn best in a structured environment.

I've learned to use a regular routine that follows the same format daily. Teaching in a predictable fashion reduces students' anxiety because they know what to expect. One student journaled, "*I can focus best when I am in a routine. When I get in a routine and I know what to expect then I can concentrate on things that are important, but If I break my routine then I worry about adjusting and I tend to loose focus on important things.*" Students repeatedly report that they appreciate classroom routines. As one put it, "*I also found it helpful that every class was structured in basically the same way. I am a person of routine and it helped me focus when I knew what was coming next throughout the hour.*"

Schedule

At-risk students find it helpful to know what's going to happen during each day's session. Some teachers write the projected schedule for the day on the board, providing students with a useful visual organizer. My students can infer the schedule from the gray sheet, which lists the day's content.

Classroom Routine

My daily classroom routine begins just before class officially starts. I return all homework assignments and quizzes from the previous day so that students receive immediate feedback on their work. My students need daily feedback on their quizzes and homework, so I correct them overnight and hand them back the next day. For a student who was absent, I also add the previous day's handouts to the materials being returned. I make sure that I remove the previous day's vocabulary quiz, so that the student doesn't see the content and can later make up the quiz. This simple routine keeps every student up to date.

Warm-up activity. At the high school or elementary school level, I suggest starting each class with a warm-up activity. Some teachers begin with an activity written on the board. The students know that, when they enter the room, they are to get out some paper and start working on the assignment. Such opening assignments could include writing about something taught the previous day in class, writing a description of a picture, or filling in cartoonish speech balloons. You can collect these and grade them, or circulate and look quickly at each one and put a stamp or check mark at the top of the page, indicating that it is acceptable. This kind of activity is especially good for helping students make the transition into the classroom from whatever was happening in their lives immediately before class.

Review of new vocabulary words. I usually begin class with a review of the vocabulary words that need to be learned for the next day. I never assume that my students will automatically figure out the pronunciation of new words on their own, so I dedicate class time daily for this. I ask students to look at the new words on their vocabulary sheets as I pronounce them, and as they then repeat them. Seeing the words, hearing them, and then saying them immediately taps into visual, auditory, and kinesthetic modes of learning. Students who simply repeat without looking at the vocabulary words tend to score lower on quizzes. Students also work on vocabulary pronunciation with their tutors weekly. They can listen to it online as well.

Review of current vocabulary words and daily quiz. After the next day's words are finished, we take up the current day's words so that they are freshest in the students' memories. I then put up an overhead of the day's quiz and give students a half page of scratch paper. If the word is in English, students write the French word, and vice versa. They must also give the right gender of nouns and correct punctuation and capitalization. As students complete their quiz, they turn it upside down. Using the target language, I confirm that everyone has finished. Students then exchange papers and correct each other's work. I elicit from students the correct answer for each word or phrase and then write it clearly on the overhead with an erasable pen. I give partial credit for incorrect genders or if a misspelled word or phrase is still recognizable. Where there are errors, graders are to write in the correct answers. Students write the proper grade on their classmate's quiz, which is handed back to the quiz taker before being handed in to me. I check the quizzes over after class and record the grades. In correcting each other's quizzes, students tend to miss little things, so I always review the quizzes afterward. Sometimes students grade too generously or harshly. After looking them over, I assign a final grade. Daily quizzes are based on approximately ten to twelve words or phrases, grouped thematically. Each quiz is generally worth about 4 or 5 points out of a semester total of 175–200 points.

Collection of homework, journals, and other assigned work. Students next turn in their written homework for the day along with any journals, corrected tests, and assignments due that day. Occasionally when an exercise has been particularly hard for students, I take a few minutes to go over the difficult parts of the exercise before students hand them in so that they don't get too frustrated making corrections. Sometimes we begin these difficult exercises together at the end of the previous day's class, after the lesson has been taught. This gives students a chance to know how to begin and generally makes the assignment go more smoothly at home. Besides that, I generally don't use my "precious" class time for things students can do on their own.

Review of previous day's grammar. I next review the previous day's grammar lesson. As a rule, I review material before introducing new information. Normally I ask students to teach it back to me. I do this by taking out a blank overhead transparency, writing the topic on it, and then eliciting from the students whatever they can remember about that topic. Little by little, they produce the major points, thereby giving everyone a brief synopsis of the previous day's lesson. Students appreciate this. One student journaled, *"My concentration on the grammar lessons and the lesson reviews is crucial for how I score on tests and quizzes."* Doing a quick review is also useful for students who were absent the previous day, serving as a minilesson of missed content. Even though absent students receive the daily gray handout when they return to class, they benefit from seeing a concise review of the previous day's lesson.

Presentation of new lesson. After reviewing the previous day's concept, I begin a new lesson. I've discovered that it's important not to leave new material until the end of class, when students' focus is waning. Specific lessons lend themselves better to inductive or deductive approaches. My lesson never lasts too long, since students with attention issues tend to fade out quickly. During my school's intensive January term, when class sessions last three hours daily, I give students one or two brain recesses.[2] I have the students stand up, stretch, take a quick walk down the hallway to get a drink from the water fountain—two or three minutes to get the blood moving again so that students can focus for another block of time. Such a recess is especially important for students in schools that are on block scheduling.

I involve the students as much as possible during my lessons, interspersing questions (e.g., "Do you see any patterns in this new verb?"), cultural tidbits, and maybe some quick conversations on the topic. For example, if I've just taught the new verb *sortir* ("to go out"), I may ask the students in French if they're going out tonight, if they went out last night, and if so, with whom. This gives a real-life context for what they have just been taught. While I don't expect students to immediately master the verb, I do expect them to be able to recognize the question and attempt an answer.

Interacting with students also helps me monitor their comprehension during instruction. I continually survey the looks on students' faces (whether they seem puzzled or seem to be "getting it"), staying alert for student questions.

Other activities. I use remaining class time to do cultural activities from the textbook, view a video clip related to chapter content, or engage in a listening activity. If any time remains, we may sing a song or do a five-minute game* such as *Pictionnaire*.

*see resource at www.foreignlanguagesforeveryone.com

Designing Assignments Wisely

What's it like to be an at-risk student? Sometimes it's like going to a grocery store to buy something, but then forgetting, when you get to the store, what you were supposed to buy. Or it's like going to the kitchen to do something and then discovering something else that needs quick attention and doing that new task instead of the original one—which you may quickly forget in the process. This is why it's so important to give at-risk students structure for homework assignments, including breaking assignments into numerous shorter tasks and recording those tasks on paper.

Chapter Assignments

At the start of each new book chapter, I give students several purple pages—handouts of written directions for the entire chapter so they know from day to day what they have to do for homework. (I always print the homework handouts* on purple paper so that students know immediately what they are and where they should go in their binders.*) I provide explicit instructions in a bulleted checklist format—the vocabulary words they are to study, the textbook sections they are to read (grammar explanations, culture notes, etc.), and the exercises they are to do from the textbook and the workbook. I also indicate which exercises students must correct with an answer key—and those that need to be written out and handed in. I don't generally give oral directions, unless a given assignment is particularly difficult.

Form and Frequency of Assignments

With advances in computer technology, some teachers like to put homework assignments online, but I believe that this might not be the best idea for students with attention difficulties. First, students would have to remember to go to the website—and then actually go there. They would have to avoid getting distracted by e-mail, Twitter, Facebook, and who knows what else. They would also have to print or copy down the directions accurately. Some students can do this well, but for others there are too many potential distractions. I suggest giving students their homework a whole chapter at a time, if at all possible, or a week at a time, or, at the very least, in a daily sheet with that day's assignment. If your school has a policy about putting homework on a website, then you can always do that in addition to the paper copy.

Order of Homework Completion

I ask students to do their homework in the order in which it is listed on the day's assignment, since there is a logical sequence involved. Vocabulary words can be studied before, after, or during the rest of the homework assignment. Many students study the words right before going to sleep in order to embed the words into their memory.[3] They also review the words right before the daily quiz.

Testing for Learning

One of the great myths that new teachers and students tend to hold is that preparing a valid, reliable, fair test is quick and easy. Those of us who have been in education for a long time know that the opposite is true. Preparing good tests* takes a lot of time and effort! In order for students to demonstrate what they've learned—not just what they haven't learned—tests have to be crafted carefully. They should never be purposely tricky; such exams are a sure means of irritating students and diminishing their motivation as well as performance. The weighting of each exercise should reflect the emphasis given in the classroom to the areas of teaching and learning that are reflected in the exercise. Tests should also assess the five areas of language development: reading, writing, speaking, listening, and culture.[4] Students should never be required to do an exercise on a test that they have never done before, either in class or for homework. I structure all chapter tests similarly in order to reduce students' fears.

Test Anxiety

Many students have a history of test anxiety. One of my students journaled, *"The other frustration is when I'm taking a test or quiz and I just can't seem to recall vocabulary correctly or something . . . but I was told that I would always have that because of my memory problem."* A severely dyslexic student with apparent memory issues wrote, *"I did do ok on a few things* [on the test] *but it seems like my mind always goes blank and I can't think. It's always stuff I need to know. How convenient!"* Some students do indeed freak out when they have to take an exam, regardless of their preparation. Forgetting things under pressure is a common phenomenon among at-risk students. It's sometimes called "brain freeze."

One highly anxious student wrote a lengthy journal entry, describing preparation for a test:

* see resource at www.foreignlanguagesforeveryone.com

> *I started studying for this test in advance, and let me tell you, I shock even myself with this one. I started studying and preparing for the test last Thursday! Yes, that's early for me considering I have other projects and such due that I need to work on . . . but I am so nervous for this test. . . . I tried to re-write important things that I need to imbed into my brain. By the time we were given the practice test to be due today, I took it and began to worry even more. I was having problems with deciding whether an event/action was* imparfait *or P.C.* [two different past tenses in French]. *Then, I wanted to add etre or avoir to even the imparfait conjugations.*

The latter comment nicely exemplifies how anxiety affects learning by mixing up things in the student's mind.

But there is hope for students when instructors work carefully to help relieve their anxieties. One of my students journaled, *"I think my study habits are really paying off, and I am relieved that I have gotten over my test anxiety in this class."* Another increasingly self-confident student revealed, *"In the beginning of the year it was hard for me to actually get the test finished in the 50 minute class period. This semester I have become accustom to taking the tests and I know that I should put the bulk of the testing time into certain sections of the test."*

During a test, I often observe signs of students' anxiety or attention-deficit hyperactivity disorder (ADHD): legs swinging back and forth, tapping of hands or feet, heavy sighs, frantic and panicked looks, blotchy faces, and sometimes a kind of "shutdown" in which the student seems incapable of moving ahead. When I see the last sign, I will quietly go to that student and encourage the student to take a deep breath (because students sometimes forget to breathe when they're anxious). I also encourage them to rely on the hard studying and daily work they've done. A student journaled, *"When taking the test take the professor's advice: take a deep breath, say a prayer, and be confident in what you know."* Sometimes I simply suggest that a student move to a different section of the test and come back later to the one that's frustrating them. In any case, I remain calm, confident, and encouraging on the student's behalf.

Testing Procedures

At the start of each test, I give students about five minutes to quickly jot down any memorized verbs or charts that are still fresh in their minds.

Students can then refer back to them during the test, especially if anxiety and stress have muddled things in their brain somewhat. This simple practice immediately reduces some students' anxiety.

Test Content

I begin each test with a listening activity. For students who have weak auditory processing skills, this is very difficult. One student wrote the following about the listening section of test: "*I was so frustrated, because it was going so incredibly fast and I could not even pick up the words I though I would be able to. The second time it was played through I got a few answers, but there was still about three that I had no idea on. Even the sentences that we have to answer were hard. I was frustrated because it was not as if I could not answer the questions, it is just impossible to do so when I do not even know what the questions were saying.*"

I encourage students to carefully read the context of the text they're about to hear (given in the heading of each exercise), and review the questions they're being asked to answer. I play the listening section one time in its entirety. Then I do it a second time, stopping in crucial spots, so that students can replay in their minds what was just said. Students appreciate the fact that I stop the speech stream by stopping the spoken text. A student journaled, "*It's good though that you understand and know how hard it is that you will replay it and break it up for us so we have time to think and make connections. . . . [O]therwise I would fail the whole section.*" In rare circumstances when the audio portion seems to be unclear, I repeat the salient part of the spoken text. I don't want students to get used to having me do that for them, however, because then they would assume that they don't really have to listen carefully on their own the first time through.

The next test activity usually requires students to write out complete-sentence responses in French to questions that I pose in French. One-word answers—such as "Yes" or "No" or "At ten o'clock"—are incomplete sentences. Students must answer with a sentence that contains a subject and a verb (e.g., "Yes, I studied yesterday" or "I get home at ten o'clock"). I encourage them to listen carefully to the tense of the verb used, so as to answer appropriately. If students have difficulty with this type of test exercise, I recommend they use a strategy such as jotting down as much of the question as they can and then returning to it later. I suggest they keep their answer simple and to the point in order to avoid introducing extraneous errors—although they will lose few, if any, points for longer answers. For instance, if the question posed is "*Qu'est-ce que vous avez fait hier soir?*" ("What did you do last night?"), there is no need to include "last night" in their response. Students are expected to answer truthfully and logically. So if they're asked, "How old is your mother?" they need to provide an accurate answer, such as, "She is forty-nine years old." They should not just contrive a number that they do know how to write. As to logical answers, if the question is something like, "What would you do if you found a million dollars?," a logical answer might be, "I would buy a new car," but probably not, "I would work."[5]

Students sometimes do a dictation exercise. I read sentences with missing words to them, and they fill in the blanks with the missing words. In order to fill in the blanks logically, students must pay close attention to the context around the blanks and translate the sentences. For example, in the sentence, "*Je vais aller au cinéma*" ("I am going to go to the movies"), the verb *aller* will have a different ending than in the sentence, "*Je suis allé au cinéma*" ("I went to the movies"), even though *aller* and *allé* sound exactly the same. Therefore, in order to give the correct spelling, the students need to puzzle out the meaning of the entire sentence.

The next several exercises focus on the grammatical concepts contained in the relevant chapter. I follow these with a reading activity in which students must answer questions in English to demonstrate they have grasped the main content of the written text. Students readily identify many written cognates—and usually do well on reading exercises. But spoken cognates are often unrecognizable to at-risk students. Passages are as culturally authentic as possible and may include such items as a restaurant menu, a magazine article on housing in France, a poem, a travel brochure, or instructions on a bottle of medicine. I don't expect students to understand every word, but they should be able to get the gist of the text and answer the questions appropriately.

The final test exercise, based on culture, is usually worth about 10 percent of the test grade. I give it this much weight for several reasons. First, culture is a key ingredient to learning a second language, including understanding people from the target culture. Second, students find culture interesting and remember it well. Third, any student can do well on this part of the test regardless of learning difficulties. Fourth, I spend considerable class time on culture. Finally, studying culture is a beneficial way for students to reflect on differences between their own culture and the target culture. For instance, I might ask students to write a paragraph in English on whether they would prefer to be a student in a French or American educational system. Regardless of which system they would prefer, they need to know the differences and similarities between cultures in order to answer the question satisfactorily.

Presenting Content

Many aspects of teaching at-risk students need careful thought and preparation. I work hard at presenting new content in a way that will register firmly in students' minds so they can retrieve it when needed. This is why I limit how much I present at one time. I develop concepts in a spiral-like fashion—from the simple to the more complex—connecting to what they already know and continuing to build on that developing foundation. I also break things down into small, bite-sized pieces. Then I bring these concepts back repeatedly until they become automatic.

Using Logical Order of Concepts with Limited Scope

Another aspect of my structured teaching methodology is to present new grammar in a logical order while limiting the quantity of new content presented in each class session. I introduce no more than one or two new concepts in a given class period. I also attend carefully to the logical sequencing of material, ensuring that a concept begins simply and is developed gradually. For instance, before addressing adjective placement (before or after the noun), I define what an adjective is and explain that students need to recall that adjectives must agree in number and gender with the noun they're modifying. At a slightly higher level of instruction, before students can learn the formation of the comparative (e.g., "bigger") and superlative ("biggest") forms of adjectives, they need to understand the placement of adjectives. This structured spiraling of concepts must be done carefully, so that each one can build on those that came before.

Activating Prior Knowledge

Good educational practice first activates a student's prior knowledge about something before building on that knowledge. This is sometimes called "cognitive Velcro" because a new concept is fastened to something students already know before expanding their knowledge. Mel Levine describes a learner with an "active" mind as one who keeps "connecting new ideas to what she already knows. No sooner does an active mind take in information than it lets that new bit of knowledge ring bells, forming associations and linkages with preexisting knowledge or experience."[6] Since many of my students have difficulty making these connections, I help them bridge this gap. For example, before teaching the use of the two French past tenses (*Passé Composé* and *Imparfait*) together in a sentence or in a paragraph, I remind them how these verb tenses are formed and translated into English. Then I can more successfully add the new linguistic information to their existing knowledge. I aim to avoid assuming that students might quickly recall prior knowledge without it being activated.

Working with Small, Manageable Chunks

Teaching at-risk students requires breaking down content into small, manageable chunks.[7] As I indicated earlier, this is why I provide homework assignments in bulleted, step-by-step fashion; students then can stay on track, in the right order, and simply check off the little box in front of each piece when they have completed it. Also, I wouldn't give students a fifty-word vocabulary quiz at the end of the week. Instead I assign ten to twelve words or phrases for students to study every day after class. Then I give them a quiz on that material in the subsequent class session.

Breaking the long word lists down is vitally important. At-risk students who failed at a foreign language frequently cite their inability to master large lists of words when quizzes were given only weekly. While students don't fully like daily vocabulary quizzes, they acknowledge their value. One of my students said, *"Vocabulary quizzes help me maintain so I am not overwhelmed at the test and I have one less thing to study because I already know them all."*

Repeating and Reviewing Frequently

I will only briefly discuss here the importance of frequent repetition and review because I offer more on the topic in chapter 6, especially with regard to the importance of regular repetition of vocabulary. Research shows that in order for something to become firmly embedded in a person's memory it must be frequently repeated until it becomes automatic.[8]

While there is very limited class time during an academic year to repeat things intensively, some things do need to be reviewed and repeated regularly. One example of this in my class is the repetition of classroom directives, such as *"Tournez à la page cinq"* ("Turn to page five") and *"Passez-moi vos devoirs et vos corrections"* ("Pass me your homework and your corrections."). As students are completing their daily vocabulary quiz, I ask them, *"Fini? Qui n'a pas fini?"* ("Finished? Who hasn't finished?") By the time I teach the grammatical concept of negative question formation in the *Passé Composé*, they have heard this phrase numerous times already; they now have a well-embedded model sentence in their heads—one on which to base future iterations of this kind of sentence structure. When we're studying the interchangeability of *Qui* ("Who?") and *Qui est-ce qui*, ("Who is it who/that?"), I ask the postquiz question using both forms so that the students know the phrases mean exactly the same thing.

Another example is my regular review of the four "big verbs" in French: *être, avoir, aller, faire* ("to be," "to have," "to go," "to do/make"). The first two verbs are the helping verbs used to form the present perfect tense. The third one is used in the immediate future tense—what my students and I call the "gonna" tense. When I tutored Central American refugees, one asked, "What does 'gonna' mean? I keep hearing people say 'We're gonna do this or that' and I don't know what they mean!" The fourth verb is used in many common everyday phrases (especially relating to weather). It's crucial for students to be able to employ these verbs automatically. Sometimes we review them with whiteboards; other times we do a quick oral review (e.g., I have students toss a soft ball to each other and give the parts of the verb). On each test, I encourage students to write them down somewhere so they can refer back to them, as needed.

Structuring Lesson Planning*

I wonder if most teachers enjoy preparing lesson plans any more than many at-risk students enjoy learning with them. I suspect that many teachers don't prepare detailed lesson plans because they simply don't like the preparing as much as the teaching. Some instructors' plans are simply a short notation in a plan book—hardly a detailed schedule about what, when, how, and why to teach something.

* see resource at www.foreignlanguagesforeveryone.com

When it comes to teaching a foreign language to at-risk learners, how-ever, overly vague planning is a recipe for disaster. If a teacher doesn't plan details, students will have to fill in the details for themselves. This is simply too much to ask of most at-risk learners. Just as tests need to be carefully constructed, daily lesson content must be meticulously orchestrated and scrupulously organized. Even though I've been teaching for forty years, I still script my lesson plans thoroughly every day. I no longer feel the need to put a time line into my plans because I have a better sense of how long something will take and what to do if I get behind. But I still do lay out all the steps, transitions, and grammatical explanations. And I always include some backup activities in case there is time left over at the end of class. After each day's lesson, I evaluate the day's session, noting what worked well and what didn't, recording the things for which there wasn't enough time, and citing any changes to make in subsequent terms. This has proven invaluable for my teaching from year to year. I don't repeat exactly the same mistakes annually, but I also don't need to reinvent my lessons each year; I can delete the things for which there was insufficient time, and adapt the things that didn't work as well as expected.

Specifically, I type out all my lesson plans in a Word document that I print out and put in my binder by day. I organize them as "Day 1," "Day 2," and so on. That's how I know there are exactly fifty-two days in a four-semester-hour class! If there is an activity that I think would be nice but not essential to do, I type "If time" by it—so that I know with a glance that it's not vital. On the rare occasions that I have time left over toward the end of a class period, I quickly use the "if time" activity. When I was supervis-ing student teachers years ago, I strongly recommended they always have a few backup activities ready, especially since they often ran out of things to do in class and then would stand there and wonder what to do next!

At the end of the day, after a day's lesson, I go back over the plan and note the things I did not have time for and I write "no time" in pencil on the paper lesson plan. These parts of the lesson plan then get carried over to the next day; I simply copy and paste them into the next day's lesson. I leave them in the original lesson plan, but when I type that plan out the subsequent year, I add "if time" in my printed plan, in case this year I might be able to squeeze it in. If I go several years without having the time, I delete it from the plan. This works only when I can use the same textbook for several years in a row.

Visualizing in Handouts

Aligned with my goal of making learning multisensory, I always try to add a visual component to the auditory nature of the class—such as the use of color-coded paper and card stock, discussed in chapter 1. Research shows that fonts with lots of curlicues or ornamentation tend to be harder to read, although modest serifs do help most readers. I try to make all of my handouts as clear as possible in terms of font type (Times New Roman) and size (12 pt.), headings, bullets, numbering, and spacing on the page, all of which make a page easier to read. It's tempting—but bad educational practice—to use a lot of fancily designed material. PowerPoint and word processors make it so easy to cloud legibility in the name of impressive presentation.

Setting Fitting Expectations

When I was growing up in a Dutch-immigrant family, my parents always held high expectations of us children. Even though my parents completed only elementary school, we younger siblings had the privilege of attending college. Moreover, I attended schools that were founded by people who had immigrated to Canada after World War II to seek religious freedom and a better life. Even my teachers expected a lot of me and my Dutch peers.

Obviously it isn't too hard to meet low expectations, but when parents and teachers hold very high expectations, students tend to try to live up to those expectations. Children don't want to disappoint their parents, who sacrificed much on their behalf.

I, too, hold many expectations for my students. The contract* that students sign at the start of the course sequence lists a number of those expectations, such as active participation, good communication with me about issues they have, and completion of homework assignments. In chapter 7, I discuss ways to help students take responsibility for their own learning.

For now, I'd like to emphasize how important it is especially for at-risk students to know that they must keep their work organized. This is a major challenge for some of them, especially those who struggle with attention

* see resource at www.foreignlanguagesforeveryone.com

or sequencing issues. Levine addresses the difficulties that some students' minds have in organizing and sequencing various inputs; they lack spatial organization and thus often struggle in their management of time and materials.[9] When at-risk students learn how to address such issues in their studies, they gain considerable self-esteem and self-confidence—which in turn helps them to transfer their new skills to other parts of their lives.

At the beginning of my classes, some students lack metacognitive awareness of their weakness in organization and sequencing. So in order to help them help themselves, I give them strict parameters for keeping track of their course materials and homework assignments. Spanish instructor Becky Kissinger even takes a few minutes of class time each semester to help her at-risk students clean out their binders—guiding them on what to keep or recycle. I also give students a *Devoirs* ("Homework") folder with pockets in the front and back to help them keep track of corrected and still-to-be-corrected homework.

As I mentioned, I require my students to get and use a three-ring binder* with tab inserts—one insert for each kind of course handout. At the end of the first week of class during first semester, I check their binders to make sure each student has all the necessary organizational materials. The homework assignment requires students to set up their course binders with all the "bells and whistles" for the next day. One student called me at home for clarification. This student took nearly everything literally—with little sense of metaphor, irony, exaggeration, and humor. As the year progressed, I noticed possible red flags for autism-spectrum issues and recommended further testing.

Students have noted in their journals that the organizational skills they developed in my French class also helped them with other classes. One student wrote,

> I have been quite pleased with my progress in the new language. My prog-
> ress has been due in large part to the structure and organization of the
> class. The color-coated binder system has been really helpful. Rarely am I
> this organized, especially about anything school related. I can keep things
> at home organized, especially anything that I am interested in. But when
> it comes to school I am nearly hopeless. That lack of organization really
> buried me in Spanish with all the sheets that are handed out in language

> *class. However, so far in French 111 I know where everything is, notes assignments, and even miscellaneous things that I almost always lose. The system has been benefitting me greatly.*

This was written by a disorganized student with a tattered backpack who was always losing, missing, and forgetting things. The student's strengths included being a natural leader in class and bringing out others' positive traits. Maybe my class was a factor in the student's decision to purchase a new backpack during the term.

Journal entries often show me how a structured environment helps at-risk students to be successful by helping them organize things in their brains. One journaled,

> *Organization in this class is really invaluable. Prof. K. insists on some measure of organization in the beginning of the semester by checking folders for dividers. This seemed rather silly at first, but I came to find out that when it comes test time and you need to look back at all the gray sheets and vocab and who knows how many other hand-outs then you end up very, very thankful that you keep everything neat and organized. I think that good organization in the folder also helps to better organize things in my brain and this too is very helpful around test time.*

The Value of Providing Parameters

At-risk students can more easily and enjoyably learn a second language when the instructor helps them keep track of their work. One of my students journaled, *"I really like that the class is very structured and orderly. It really keeps my attention the way we are always doing something, moving from item to item, and staying involved."* This student insightfully noted the correlations among time management, organization, and mental processes. A structured classroom environment and organized course materials give students the healthy boundaries they need to be successful. This just might have been one of those eager and friendly students who first came into my classroom with great excitement but then had to borrow a pen and rummage in a backpack for that mustard-covered homework assignment.

*see resource at www.foreignlanguagesforeveryone.com

3

Getting to Know Students through a Survey

I've spent most of my entire life reflecting on what kind of learner I am and how I can be more efficient and productive. I think that's just my nature. When I worked as an office assistant to pay my way through college, I'd always try to figure out a better way to do a given job to achieve better results. When I was studying French, Latin, or German, I was continually strategizing about how to remember things—often saying words and phrases over and over in my head, translating signs I saw, or theorizing how to translate a phrase I had heard in English into the target language. I'd describe myself as having a high level of metacognitive awareness, which is very helpful in foreign-language learning—in any kind of learning, for that matter.

Most of my students need help in the area of metacognition. Many of them think creatively and easily see the big picture, but have a hard time carrying out the specifics of their brilliant ideas. Some of them have difficulty following directions in a step-by-step manner (like some of us have when trying to put together an allegedly easy-to-assemble product). They can't always break down a large project into its component steps. They often postpone getting started. Some of them struggle with remembering things (like deadlines, appointments, or where they put their keys), and only a few of them have devised helpful memory devices. Some use their cell phones to send themselves reminders; others write reminders on their hand*—employing tactile and visual modes. I like writing down items and then checking them off my list.

I greatly admire Temple Grandin, a well-known animal scientist and autism self-advocate. She knows precisely how she learns best and is a wonderful advocate for people with different kinds of minds. She reminds us all that our world needs these many different kinds of people. I also believe that all of us benefit from people who know how their minds function so that they can use their mental abilities more fittingly and effectively in particular situations. In this chapter, I look closely at metacognition—at how we and our students can learn to think about our thinking, especially in order to become better teachers and learners. I focus on how language teachers can help students benefit from a better understanding of themselves and how their minds work. I first review in some depth the important research on metacognition and language learning—important literature not usually addressed extensively at conferences. Then I show how to use a four-page, first-day questionnaire as a valuable metacognitive tool to make foreign-language learning significantly more accessible for all students. In the next chapter, I add another helpful metacognitive tool—the biweekly self-reflective journal.

Investigating the whole realm of metacognition with my students reminds me that my attitude toward my students is critically important. Education-affirming metacognition requires a hospitable educational environment in which self-knowledge is openly valued. This is partly why one essential element of good teaching practice is creating an environment where all students come to know that they have a distinct place in the learning community. Parker J. Palmer, influential author of such important educational works as *To Know as We Are Known* and *The Courage to Teach*, suggests that "real learning does not happen until students are brought into relationship with the teacher, with each other, and with the subject. We cannot learn deeply and well until a community of learning is created in the classroom."[1] Henri J. Nouwen, a Dutch-born Catholic priest and the author of many books about the spiritual life, maintains that "when we look at teaching in terms of hospitality, we can say that the teacher is called upon to create for his students a free and fearless space where mental and emotional development can take place."[2] Both writers address the importance of getting to know individual students in their

* see resource at www.foreignlanguagesforeveryone.com

own diversity. I've learned that teaching and employing metacognition helps establish such open, affirming self-knowledge for the sake of more effective and enjoyable foreign-language study.

Considering Metacognition Research

I use the term "metacognition" to refer to thinking about cognition—or thinking about thinking. As students learn their own cognitive strengths and weaknesses, they increasingly comprehend how they can learn most effectively. In order for students to grow in this self-understanding, they need to deeply reflect on their learning. As I explain below, I successfully use questionnaires and journals to help students gain such understanding of their own cognition.

According to German psychological researchers Franz E. Weinert and Rainer H. Kluwe, metacognition refers to "cognition about cognition, and means knowledge about one's own thinking, and cognitive activity."[3] Scott G. Paris and Peter Winograd, who have researched the impact of metacognitive beliefs on learners, conclude that metacognitive "beliefs, judgments, and choices enable students to become independent learners."[4]

John H. Flavell, the pioneer in the study of metacognitive effects on learning, identifies three kinds of metacognitive knowledge: *person knowledge, task knowledge*, and *strategy knowledge*.[5] Larry Vandergrift, who taught high school French for twenty years before pursuing graduate work and conducting important language research, says that person knowledge "includes knowledge of the cognitive and affective factors that facilitate learning and what learners know about themselves as learners." He contends that person knowledge can help students "become active participants in their own learning, rather than passive recipients of instruction. . . . Students are encouraged to reflect on their performance, to evaluate its success, to make choices, and to look for ways to improve, thereby redirecting their learning."[6] This is especially true for weak language learners who have very low self-efficacy and who don't understand themselves well as learners.[7]

Douglas J. Palmer, dean of the College of Education and Human Development at Texas A&M University, and his colleague Ernest T. Goetz, a distinguished research fellow in educational psychology, concluded years ago that students who perceive themselves as "incompetent may be disinclined to attempt the use of any strategy."[8] In other words, self-perception is a critical factor in student motivation. I agree. My students generally come to class with extremely low self-efficacy. Having failed previously, they believe that they will fall short again. They are caught in a spiral of self-fulfilling failure before they set foot in my classroom.

In her seminal work on multisensory structured metacognitive foreign-language instruction, Elke Schneider of Winthrop University examined how students might gain *metalinguistic* awareness, in particular, by reflecting on language rather than on self-knowledge.[9] While I agree on the importance of such metalinguistic awareness, I focus in this chapter on a broader definition of metacognition, which includes issues such as overall self-regulation and self-efficacy. I believe that such broader metacognition helps students establish the basic self-understanding that they need to achieve higher academic performance overall—not just in language learning. In an ideal educational situation, students would have gained such understanding before foreign-language study. Leonore Ganschow and Richard L. Sparks, longtime leaders in the research, suggest that "at-risk learners lack metacognitive skills, i.e., ability to reflect on language and to use self-correction strategies without explicit instruction."[10]

Students' perceptions of language learning are also important when they begin foreign-language study. Suzanne Graham, who directs research for the Institute of Education at the University of Reading in Britain, found that "both effective learner strategy use and motivational maintenance are influenced by learners' metacognitive knowledge or beliefs about language learning. Thus an understanding of learners' beliefs about foreign-language learning has implications for classroom instruction and interaction with learners."[11]

In her overview of metacognition, educational psychologist Jennifer A. Livingston concluded that "although most individuals of normal intelligence engage in metacognitive regulation when confronted with an effortful cognitive task, some are more metacognitive than others. Those with greater metacognitive abilities tend to be more successful in their cognitive endeavors. The good news is that individuals can learn how to better regulate their cognitive activities."[12] In this chapter, I build on this good news by explaining one strategy in my metacognitive tool kit: a questionnaire. I use this questionnaire, along with the student journal I discuss in the next chapter, to help students become successful and autonomous language learners who understand how their brains work.

Surveying Students with a Questionnaire

I've found that the best way to get an initial read on my students is to have them fill out a first-day questionnaire.* This metacognitive tool not only requests basic factual information; it also taps into students' perceptions of themselves as learners. As with all student transparency, the questionnaire needs to be used carefully, sensitively, and in tune with legal and ethical guidelines about privacy.

All of my students enter my classroom convinced that foreign-language learning will be difficult for them personally. Many have tried in the past and failed; now they have to put themselves through the painful experience once again! Based on an examination of the research, Dorcas Francisco, who taught Spanish in an inclusion classroom and later instructed students in a special-education school, concluded that "students classified as learning disabled are equally motivated in learning foreign languages, but their self-perception as low achievers often leads to classroom anxiety and eventual loss of motivation."[13] I completely agree.

If students perceive themselves as being poor learners in general, and especially poor foreign-language learners, they're likely to meet their low self-expectations. Barry J. Zimmerman and Albert Bandura, pioneering researchers in educational psychology, suggest that "people who harbor self-doubts about their capabilities are easily dissuaded by obstacles or failures. Those who are assured of their capabilities intensify their efforts when they fail to achieve what they seek, and they persist until they succeed."[14] Many of my students fit that description. They have been admitted into my sequence because of prior failures at foreign-language learning, or they were advised to avoid even attempting a second language.

In order to gain a snapshot of my students' questionnaire responses, I examined one full year's (2005–6) responses for all twenty-nine students—fifteen males and fourteen females whose average age was twenty years and one month.[15] Students reported their own weaknesses in auditory processing, spatial and sequential processing, memory, attention, and social thinking, as well as difficulties such as dyslexia and dysgraphia.

Since I distribute the questionnaire on the first day of class, students don't know and trust me yet. So I tell them that everything on it will be kept confidential. Students fill it out at home and bring it back the next day. Presumably they will understate self-reported learning problems. Imagine beginning a foreign-language course with this group!

Each of my students has already gone through a long process* (including permission for release of personal information from our learning-disabilities office) in order to be considered for admission into the sequence. Student self-reports are not hard data, so I look for common themes across student responses. My one-year analysis was consistent with student responses over many years.

Observant readers can pick up a lot from such a questionnaire. For instance, I look for spelling errors and the nature of these errors, and the seriousness with which the student completes the questionnaire, including whether they seemed to put in time to complete it or may have quickly completed it at the last minute. I also consider handwriting style—and what it might say about a student. Very few of my students use cursive; most print, and some only in capitals. I prefer they use cursive, but apparently some schools no longer require it. Perhaps mastering cursive is too great a demand on my students' cognitive and fine-motor abilities. In any case, many continue to print.[16] The following overarching topics emerge from my analysis of survey results:

- Memory issues (difficulties and strategies)
- Failure at foreign-language learning
- Native-language skills in the areas of spelling, grammar, reading, and listening
- Organization and sequencing skills
- Personal characteristics and study habits
- Issues of self-efficacy and intellectual self-esteem

Many of the themes addressed in my questionnaire relate directly to students' abilities to learn a foreign language. We can better serve students if we know that they have struggled with memorizing, failed previously at a foreign language, or had difficulties with language skills in their native

*see resource at www.foreignlanguagesforeveryone.com

tongues. Similarly, we can teach more effectively if we determine that our students might be weak at certain life skills. Perhaps most importantly, the questionnaire can help us determine the type and level of student fears about mastering another language. The questionnaire is one very helpful means for us and our students to begin our learning journey together by considering some issues that need to be examined and discussed for future success. I have learned over the years that the more I know about who my students are as distinct persons and what they bring into our class community, the better able I am to help them succeed.

Understanding the Basic Questionnaire Topics

Since I've found that this relatively simple metacognitive tool can convey a lot of helpful foreign-language study information, I will walk you through the questionnaire section by section, explaining why questions are included, commenting on the questions, and discussing what can be learned from each section.

Basic Information

The questionnaire—see supplement 2 in the back of this book or download an editable version from my website*—begins with some basic factual information, such as the student's full name and the name they would like to use in the class with me and other students. Knowing a student's preferred name helps me connect with them personally. When students tell something to help me remember who they are, their answers provide insights into their self-perceptions—especially what they think is important about themselves, perhaps even a key to their self-identity. Here are some examples:

- "I'm tall and I play tennis." (At my institution, this isn't unusual.)
- "I am driven to make progress." (This might indicate a type-A personality or some compulsive issues.)
- "I have diabetes." (This is good to know in case of a diabetic incident in class.)
- "I am a perfectionist—I am either really clean or really messy." (This was written in perfect script.)

Students provide their contact information, class level, and academic majors and minors. Many are in professional programs, such as business and education. I get few nursing and engineering majors, whose programs require a minimum amount of foreign-language study in high school for college admission. Students' biographical information gives me some idea of their geographical and educational background. Because family background can be touchy and complicated, this question is purposely open ended, making it clear that they can provide as much or as little information as they wish. For some students, this is a highly sensitive area. For instance, one student was raised by an aunt and uncle because biological parents had been abusive.

Career Goals

I ask students to address their career goals. Interestingly, many aspire to do some kind of hands-on work or pursue a creative endeavor, or seek to be special education teachers—probably because they understand the struggles of students with learning disabilities.

Leisure-Time Activities

The next section deals with students' leisure time. They tend to enjoy such activities as sports, hanging out with friends, watching TV or YouTube, and playing video games. Many don't like to read in their spare time, except possibly popular magazines rather than books. This isn't surprising, since many students with learning disabilities have language-processing difficulties that make reading a chore rather than a pleasure.

Gaining, Giving, and Goals

In response to my question about what they hope to gain from taking the sequence, many students say "knowledge about a different culture and language," "credit," or "a decent grade." A very common reply is something like this: "To be honest, I hope only to fulfill the foreign-language requirement. Anything more is a bonus." However, a few of my students say they really want to learn French: "Learn the language, and feel like I actually learned something from the class." One metacognitively self-aware student wrote, "I hope to learn how to learn a language and I hope to learn French."

I also ask what students hope to give to the class, including their goals for the class. Here I'm trying to help my students see that, even though they are individual learners, they are also part of a community of learners. Parker J. Palmer writes, "It is said that all of us together are smarter than any one of us alone."[17] I hope that over the course of the year the students will increasingly realize that they have certain educational obligations to further each others' learning. This means that if one student is absent, every student is somewhat diminished, because the group is missing that student's contributions. I articulate this to students on the first day of class. I believe that students learn best in an environment where they have a stake in being there—where they can *get* something but also *give* something. Students' goals for the course can be personal, educational, or other, but the question forces them to think about what they hope to achieve and to articulate some goals toward which they will work. The questionnaire gives me a natural way of raising this pedagogical topic.

Expectations of Course

My institution is a large, undergraduate, Christian liberal arts college in the Reformed Protestant tradition. Since the students elect to attend such an institution, they generally share some assumptions about the importance of communal learning for the common good—not just taking courses for personal gain. But I ask students how they expect French to be taught differently than it might be taught at a nonreligious school. In a sense, this is a kind of metareligious question that provides some sense of how students might think philosophically or at least reflectively about their education. Student responses range from expecting absolutely no difference at all, to such things as reading the Bible and praying in the target language, respecting the culture, using the language to benefit others, and expecting a greater degree of care toward students.

Prior Schooling

The questionnaire then addresses prior schooling. I ask students to recall what their most- and least-favorite subjects were—and why. While some students list foreign language as their least-favorite subject, many also cite math. They say they're "terrible at math," that they find it "totally worthless, hard, and boring," or that "numbers mean nothing" to them. About science, students typically indicate that they "don't understand the concepts very easily." Some students find that subjects heavy on facts (such as history) are hard because there is "nothing to link facts together"—a comment suggesting memory difficulties. A few students say that they're bad at English—meaning that they aren't proficient at grammar. A handful of students say that their favorite subjects are English (literature or creative writing), history ("because it's just a story and you just need to place the events in order"), or science (usually biology or human anatomy, but not chemistry). An occasional student even lists math as a favorite subject. Some students' favorite subject areas are those that tap into their creativity (such as art), or those that deal with the human mind or with how people interact (such as psychology or sociology). Sometimes students leave this entire question blank, suggesting that they lack any favorite subjects; for them, school takes a great toll. Numerous students say their "brain" prevents them from mastering certain subjects, demonstrating once again the implicitly metacognitive nature of the questionnaire.

Considering the Developing Research

While following the research over the years, I regularly added related questionnaire items. The following six question topics are in that category. I hope that by including my explanation for incorporating these into the metacognitive questionnaire, I'll inspire you to monitor the research and add questions of your own. Please visit my website to share your own variations on the questionnaire.

Self-Description

The first additional question asks students to give three words to describe themselves. Generally speaking, answers fall into the following self-reported categories:

- Obsessive/perfectionist
- Happy/content/joyful
- Sporty/athletic
- Creative/artistic
- Caring/loving/understanding/loyal
- Fun/funny/goofy/crazy
- Quiet/easygoing/calm/relaxed
- Friendly

- Sincere/honest
- Procrastinator/sporadic
- Shy/passive
- Outgoing/lively/energetic/adventurous

Less-frequently reported categories include talkative, listener, hard-working, motivated, techie, bossy, observant, confident, and proud. Many students use mostly upbeat words to describe themselves. These responses contrast sharply with the negative descriptions that students use to describe their prior foreign-language experience.

Learning Style

A second added question asks students to describe how they learn best and how they would describe their learning style (e.g., visual, auditory, kinesthetic, or other). For many, the visual and kinesthetic modes are stronger than the auditory mode. Students often say that they learn best by *doing* something rather than by reading about it.

Learning Successes

The third newer question asks students to reflect on what a person who knows them well would say they excel in. I ask this question from a third-person perspective because I believe I will receive more generous answers that way. Many students seem reluctant to say positive things about themselves.

Musical Training

The fourth newer question addresses the auditory mode and students' musical training. I believe that students who have had some musical training are more likely to be stronger second-language learners. There is much research on music and foreign-language learning.[18] Katie Overy, who coestablished the Institute for Music in Human and Social Development at the University of Edinburgh, connects music lessons with dyslexic students. She writes, "In summary, this research strengthened the argument that music lessons have the potential to provide a valuable multisensory learning environment for dyslexic children. A particular advantage of music lessons as a language support tool is that they can be used at any stage of literacy development and at any age, from pre-school to high school."[19] Other scholars have drawn parallels between music and language development.[20]

Positive and Negative Learning Experiences

Newer questions five and six ask students to recall any prior schooling incident in which they were ever academically criticized or academically successful—and how such experiences made them feel. Here I'm trying to tease out a sense of students' self-esteem as learners in general and foreign-language learners in particular. I believe that if a student had a negative experience, especially in foreign-language learning, it will stick with them indefinitely until it is resolved. One student wrote, "I wish that I never had a prior experience with a language before this class because than I would not have come to it with any negative feelings." A colleague and I have wondered if such painful learning experiences could best be healed through an intentional act of forgiveness.[21]

Determining Students' Prior Learning Experiences

In trying to get a picture of my students as learners, I ask them a number of questions about their experiences in various academic areas. I'm most interested in their earlier foreign-language experiences, but I also want to know about other areas that might give me insights. Some of the questions are directly language-related (such as grammar and English). Others provide more general insights about learning. For instance, questions about a student's experience with social studies can help me determine how they respond to a discipline that often requires considerable memorization of facts. While students often say they struggle with math and science (on an earlier question about least-favorite subjects), I don't ask about those directly for fear of contributing to students' existing unease. Since there is often a correlation between struggles in learning a foreign language and in math, I can use the math questions to indirectly address likely language-learning issues. Students provide an interesting and helpful variety of answers about their prior learning experiences.

Grammar instruction. Delving into their prior learning experiences, students describe their encounters with grammar instruction, as well as how well they think they did in reading, writing, and literature classes. Many say that they were good at creative writing, at coming up with good ideas, and at analyzing literature, but they struggled to express their ideas in writing, including spelling and syntax. One student wrote, "Grammer and me just NEVER get along!! Just end up frustrated at how I can't get the paper to say what my mind sees." Another stated, "It was always hard for me to express myself on paper." Thomas R. Miles, one of the founding members of the British Dyslexia Association, believes that dyslexics have poor spelling skills and "may have all sorts of creative ideas yet find it hard to put them down on paper."[22] Many students say that they read slowly and that this makes these classes difficult. One wrote, "I was always behind, seemed to miss important things." Another added, "Reading comprehension was weak."

Social studies. Some students say that they really liked and did well in social studies. Others reply that although the subject was not horrible to study, they did have difficulty with memorization, making comments like "Specific names and dates seem to escape from memory."

Difficult subjects. I then ask students whether some subjects have remained difficult and others not. Students often reply that their strengths and weaknesses have "remained constant." One student reported, "If the teacher teaches in a visual way I do better than if the teacher just lectures without handouts." A few students indicate that their reading and/or writing have gotten better over the years, or that they have become better students overall. Others say that difficulties with grammar and spelling persist. Some students are very aware of their learning weaknesses and how to develop strategies that will help them (such as taking extra time for learning tasks).

Previous foreign-language learning. Students provide a broad range of answers when asked about any previous foreign-language learning. Most have taken one to three years of a foreign language in high school (often Spanish, but sometimes French, German, or Latin) and attempted the same language or sometimes a different language in college. Failure is common. Some performed adequately at the beginning levels, and then struggled as they got to intermediate or advanced instruction. Sparks and his colleagues similarly reported this pattern.[23] Some students managed to pass with extra credit or tutoring. A few tried several different languages over their educational careers—presumably hoping that they would do better in a new language—but were still stymied.

One student took two years of high school Spanish, and got a D+ in college Chinese before retaking it for a C–. The student got a D+ in second-semester Chinese, but eventually withdrew from the subsequent course. Claiming to have "an artistic mind (Right Brain)," the student wrote that math was the least favorite subject. This student successfully completed my sequence and graduated.

According to the literature, some students don't even realize they have a learning disability until they start a foreign language, do poorly, and then take some tests to try to determine why.[24] This isn't surprising, because many students with learning disabilities are very bright and have developed on their own some amazingly effective compensating strategies that serve them well until they encounter the confounding phonological system of a new target language.

I ask students what made previous foreign-language learning difficult. They often mention spelling, memorization, listening, and grammar. They also address the fast pace, the complexity, the lack of review, and how they often fell behind. One student wrote, "I would just get one concept down, or I was starting to, and we would move on and I would forget the old thing and get all mixed up." Many students find conjugating verbs and the different verb tenses exceedingly difficult. Many say they simply do poorly in listening activities. One student responded, "I am not an audio learner; therefore I struggled on the listening parts of quizzes and tests." Many struggle with grammar in English and find that this difficulty transfers to the foreign language. As a student put it, "English grammer alone was horrible for me—how was I suppose to do it in another language?" Many students have a hard time pronouncing words, seemingly unable to temporarily suspend their English sound system. Another difficulty for some students is the gender of words. Many students also have trouble expressing their thoughts in the target language; they have a hard time with sentence structure and the act of putting it all together to express meaning. A student revealed, "I might be a little bit dislexic so everything [was hard]." This final act of putting together the various parts of language typically is the hardest thing for most language learners, regardless of learning difficulties, but it's enormously satisfying for me and them when students like mine begin accomplishing it.

English learning. Students next rate on a scale of one (poor) to ten (excellent) their ability in English spelling, grammar, reading, and memorization. Few rate their skills highly. In terms of spelling, the questionnaires themselves attest to the fact that many are abysmal spellers. Writing about dyslexia, Miles says that "there is almost always a history of . . . inability to remember spellings."[25] Many students also rate their grammar skills quite low. They generally rate themselves fairly high in reading, although many read very slowly. My students have all had to master reading to a fairly high level in order to be admitted into college in the first place, but for many, reading is time consuming. Often memorization skills are similarly weak.

Study habits. I ask students to describe their study habits in response to three questions. When asked how many hours they study daily, students report from one or two to six and even sometimes ten hours. Most say they study between two and five hours daily. Students say they spend the most time on their harder classes. A student wrote, "If I'm interested or am doing poorly, I'll study a lot." Another responded, "I'll work days on projects I enjoy, but lack focus on difficult tasks." Not surprisingly, many students find it easier to study for subjects they enjoy. As one student revealed, "I procrastinate, whatever I am struggling with I tend to put off to the side."

Writing. Next I ask whether students consider themselves good writers. Some say that they do well on school papers—even that they're creative and they enjoy writing. Others say that they write poorly. Here are some typical responses:

- "I only use small words and it sounds like a younger child wrote it."
- "Whenever I work very hard and think I did well, teachers tell me I'm never focused and I don't make sense . . . too wordy."
- "I have good ideas but trouble expressing them."
- "I struggle with organizing my thoughts."
- "I have trouble finding the right words or organizing them correctly."

I find that when my foreign-language students write their class papers, their English writing lacks formality and succinctness; it sounds colloquial, like their casual conversations. They don't carefully proofread for style and clarity, despite specific instructions to do so. Their lack of correct punctuation sometimes leads to ambiguous meaning. All of this is in spite of the fact that they get to select their own paper topics, which should motivate them to learn about the topic. In the fall, they must write about a well-known place in Paris; during January term, they write on a geographical area of France; in the spring, they choose a famous French person.*

English pronunciation and intelligibility. In the next part of the questionnaire, students rate their English pronunciation—whether others generally understand their speech. Some students interpret this question as pertaining to their public speaking ability even though I am trying to determine—without overly directing how they might respond—whether they have any articulation problems, such as a speech impediment. Speaking can also relate to their reading skills—notably how they might be putting sounds and symbols together. For instance, they might pronounce the word "nuclear" as "nukular"—a variation that could be simply regional dialect or an indication that the student isn't reading phonetically by pronouncing the word as it is spelled. This would raise a red flag to me as to how the student might perform when trying to put a sound and symbol together in French. The issue here is more than simply the loudness, projection, or speed of speaking, although some students say they tend to speak too speedily. Some of my students have unclear English articulation and several indicated that they tend to mumble a lot. One wrote, "I often pronounce vowels incorrectly." Another student, who was extremely difficult to understand in English, reported, "Sometimes people have trouble understanding me." In this student's case, that was definitely an understatement!

Many of my students never learned to sound out words—perhaps because of the whole language–versus–phonics debate in elementary education. Educators have to assume that some students are taught to read by whole word recognition (*whole language*) rather than by connecting sound and symbol (*phonics*).

Factual memorization and mathematical calculations. Next, students rate their ability to memorize numbers, dates, names, days of the week,

* see resource at www.foreignlanguagesforeveryone.com

and months of the year. Some struggle with sequential memory, such as remembering such lists and what order they come in. Many recount having difficulty remembering dates, phone numbers, and names. Here are some typical comments:

- "This would be where my learning disability affects me directly."
- "It is hard for me to control what I remember."
- "Numbers I can recall, all else is poor."
- One student suggested that wearing name tags would be a big help. About remembering the months of the year, the student said, "I still have to say [them] in order to know where they go. Same with the alphabet."
- A student with "horrible" memory issues wrote, "I just had to ask my roommate what our phone number was and I lived here last semester."
- Several students said that they had good ability with short-term memorization, "but not with long-term memorization."

My students often struggle with basic arithmetic. If they need to estimate on a test how much money a French lunch for their family would cost, they sometimes ask to use a calculator.

Basic memory and routine life-organization skills. Students often candidly report that they routinely forget and are regularly late for appointments and classes. I ask them whether they resort to writing things on their hands to remember them, but a quick look at students' hands reveals that many use this strategy—even if they don't remember to check their hands!*

I ask about sense of direction, of left/right, and of north/south/east/west, and whether students can read a map upside down. Many are directionally challenged. They have a hard time distinguishing left from right and are unsure of the points on a compass. They get lost easily. They can use a map if it's oriented in the direction they are facing.

Attention-deficit issues. I included the earlier question about keeping appointments and the next three questions after reading a *New York Times* article about attention-deficit hyperactivity disorder (ADHD) among adults in the workplace.[26] Students with attention difficulties often procrastinate—hence the question about whether they avoid or delay getting started on a task that requires considerable thought. The second question asks students if they often fidget or squirm with their hands or feet when they have to sit for a long time. A quick glance around my classroom, especially during a test, is evidence that many students have a hard time sitting still. I see knees bumping together, feet bouncing up and down, and hands tapping on desks. The third question asks students if they ever feel overly active and compelled to do things—as if they were being driven by a motor. Many students exhibit this tendency toward hyperactivity. Research suggests that allowing students to sit on a large rubber ball in class helps them stay focused.[27]

Sensory strengths and weaknesses. My son-in-law once came home with a beautiful new sweater. My daughter was shocked at the color and said, "Did you really buy yourself a pink sweater?" "Pink!" he replied. "I thought it was gray!" I ask students about color blindness, because all homework assignments are graded in specific colors—first in red, then in green, and then in other colors. If students can't see color variations, they will have a hard time figuring out which homework errors they still need to correct for full credit. Students with color blindness often do better with deep rather than pastel colors.

I also ask students about their sense of smell. Research has shown that the olfactory sense is one of the most powerful human senses, correlating strongly with memory and the affective domain. As I discussed in chapter 1, I believe that there is considerable potential for olfaction in multisensory teaching and learning, and I continue to think about how to incorporate it into my teaching. I wonder, too, about the effect of weak olfaction on learning.

Next I ask if they have allergies to food or other substances. These questions are purely pragmatic. Since students sometimes bring in food as a way to earn their required culture points, I need to know whether there could be an emergency if a student were highly allergic to peanuts or dairy products, for example. Some students have seasonal allergies; others are allergic to dusts, molds, and other substances. Some are highly allergic to chalk dust (myself included) or to animal dander; they shouldn't erase a chalkboard or sit next to a cat lover, whose clothes might cause an allergic reaction. Generally few students fall into this category; susceptible students normally have their allergies under control. There is also some interesting research that examines possible links between ADHD and allergies.[28]

Organizational and sequencing skills. I ask if students often misplace things like keys and papers. This can be a large area of weakness for students with attention/sequential issues. As I described earlier, one of the first things I require of my students is a binder with tab inserts. They must put color-coded class handouts in their binders daily. Because many students suffer with the issue, I inquire about students going to fetch something and then forgetting what it was. It relates to sequential perception and memory—paying careful attention in the first place and then keeping things in short-term memory until a task is completed. Students need to develop memory strategies—such as repeating something aloud or silently, while they go to fetch what they need.

When our children were in preschool, one of the segments in their "Kindergarten Readiness Test" involved giving them three tasks to do and seeing if they could complete all three without forgetting any—for example: "Walk to the blackboard. Draw a cat. Put a circle around the cat." Similarly I ask students whether they get mixed up when they're given three or more things in a row that they need to do. Again, attention and memory play major roles here, and students often need to write down the three tasks in order to remember them. This shows how the visual and tactile modes can help embed something in memory.

The *New York Times* article I mentioned earlier also led me to ask students if they have trouble wrapping up the final details of a project once the challenging parts have been done—and if they have difficulty getting things in order when they have to do a task that requires organization. Both of these questions relate to the difficulty that people with ADHD have sustaining attention so that they complete tasks successfully and on time. In the "real" world, deficits of this sort result in people losing their job, since few employers have patience for such poor performance. This question alerts me to difficulties certain students might have in completing a project or paper. If students struggle with class deadlines, I can consult their questionnaire to see how they answered.

I've found it helpful to ask if students have difficulty telling time on an analog clock. For some, this isn't a simple task because of the necessary spatial orientation and sequential perception. Few of my students wear analog watches; many no longer wear any watches; they simply consult their personal electronic devices. When students are learning foreign-language clock time, I recognize that some can't read an analog clock. A few have difficulty with a twenty-four-hour clock system (such as is used in the military and for train/plane schedules). Students normally do fine with the times up to noon, but they struggle to determine that 21:35 is also 9:35 p.m. I've seen students write out on tests the clock times one hour at a time (e.g. 13:35/1:35 p.m.; 14:35/2:45 p.m.; 15:35/3:35 p.m.) until they arrive at 21:35/9:35 p.m.

Memory strategies. Most adults have learned how to use their memories more effectively for particular work or personal tasks. When asked about their memory strategies, however, some students say that they have none. Others say that they need to repeat or write things over and over, thereby using the tactile mode. A few use mnemonic devices—acronyms for making connections. Others report using flash cards, color coordination, or pictures to remember things. One student wrote about making rhymes or songs to remember important information. That approach, as well as adding a rhythmic component (such as my daughter writing a rap tune), often works well. A student wrote about memory strategies, "Most are hard to focus on or do not work." Another wrote, "I try to but they only work part of the time." A comment like that raises the question of whether mnemonic devices might put more of a burden on memory resources than the help they provide some students. Throughout the academic year, I encourage students to journal about their memory ideas. Some develop and share wonderfully innovative memorization strategies.

Family connections. Recognizing both the importance and sensitivity of the subject, I nevertheless ask whether students have a relative who has reading or writing problems, or other learning difficulties, asking respondents to explain briefly such problems. One student wrote, "I am adopted." I presume that this meant the student didn't find the question of biological family to be germane. Many students have a parent or sibling who has a learning disability or who struggles with written language. A surprising number of students report having relatives who have been diagnosed with a learning difficulty or ADHD. Other students journal about being pretty sure a parent or sibling has ADHD or dyslexia—commonly part of a family history of learning issues.[29]

Medications. Students are quite willing to report on medication they use for learning difficulties. I ask when they take it, whether they find it helpful, and whether there are any side effects. There is a wide variety of answers here. Some students take standard medications for attention difficulties. Some have tried medication, but quit taking it because they couldn't seem to determine the right dosage or they simply didn't like side effects, such as loss of appetite and difficulty sleeping. But many find their medication quite helpful. I can usually tell when students have not taken their attention-disorder medication, especially when we do an activity that requires their full attention. Such students get very fidgety and can't even sit still to focus on the task at hand, or they space out during class.

Sleep patterns and problems. There is a growing body of research on the importance of regular sleeping patterns, especially for memory and learning.[30] So I ask how many hours students usually sleep per night, whether their sleep is restful, and whether they have a hard time falling asleep or getting up in the morning. I also ask about sleep apnea. High school and college students frequently stay up late and push themselves to get by on minimal sleep. I've had some students with deeply disturbed sleep habits who consistently have difficulty getting up in the morning. Many report they simply don't hear their alarms. They tend to be late or to miss classes completely, especially while taking an early-morning class in January. During regular semesters, I schedule midday rather than early-morning or late-afternoon classes. When I see students routinely falling asleep during class, I privately encourage them to be tested for a sleep disorder.

Handedness. My questionnaire includes a query about handedness—left, right, or ambidextrous. Left-handed students tend to have more difficulty with particular tasks, apparently because right and left brain hemispheres are used for different learning processes.[31] Distinguished educational researcher Edward A. Polloway and Tom E. C. Smith, a professor of special education, found that "left-handedness conflicts with the process of writing English from left-to-right."[32] I believe that this is partly because when left-handed students write from left to right they are constantly covering up what they have just written—and unable to quickly scan back for errors or needed changes. It can also be difficult to place the paper at a good angle visually. Compared with the general public, a much higher proportion of my students are left-handed. Polloway and Smith assert that left-handed individuals account for only 10 percent of the population, although it might be as high as 15 percent and seems to be increasing.[33] In one of my classes, a stunning one-third reported being left-handed.

Childhood. The last section of the questionnaire, a lengthy one, asks about childhood. I inquire about the age students learned to walk and to talk. Although many students can only estimate an answer, the question is meant to determine if there might have been any delays in some of the basic developmental milestones. Some recall speech therapy, for instance, even if they aren't sure precisely when. I ask specifically about any past eye-tracking therapy; such therapy reflects a growing field of research that examines correlations between eye movement and attention, or between visual perception and language.[34] I ask about ear infections, including severity and the need for tubes, since there is ample evidence documenting a strong correlation between ear infections and delays or deficits in language development.[35] A child with regular ear infections has to go through periods when speech sounds muffled and even unintelligible. It isn't surprising that such students might have had difficulty articulating sounds and received related speech therapy.

Quite a few of my students report learning to read at an age that is older than typical. In writing about dyslexia, Miles says that "there is almost always a history of lateness in learning to read."[36] Many say they found little pleasure in reading because it was difficult and took considerable time. Some indicate they were easily distracted. Students often can't remember if they learned reading via phonics, whole language, or a combination of the two, although a few recall special reading classes or tutoring. Still, quite a number enjoyed being read to. Maryanne Wolf, who directs the

Center for Reading and Language Research at Tufts University, calls reading to children while they are sitting on one's lap "the most important first precursor of literacy."[37] The fact that many students can't connect sound and symbol to sound out words leads me to suspect they probably didn't learn reading by phonics. This has major import for how they might do in sounding out foreign-language words. Many report never having been proficient spellers, demonstrating the correlation between foreign-language and native-language difficulties. Sparks and colleagues say that native-language phonological/orthographic (i.e., sound and sound/symbol learning) difficulties "play an important role in distinguishing good and poor language learners. . . ."[38] This is unquestionably true for my students.

A student told me that, after taking my yearlong multisensory sequence, the student's father noticed improvement in the offspring's ability to read English aloud (i.e., to put sound and symbol together). The two of them concluded that it must have been due to my French sequence—presumably because of my intensive focus on phonology, thereby demonstrating a reverse carryover from a foreign to a native language.

My final childhood question focuses on concussions or head injuries. Head trauma can indicate damage to cognitive functioning. Sports such as football and soccer have a high incidence of traumatic brain injury (TBI), especially if a child continues playing before healing. Mitchell Rosenthal, a distinguished professor of physical medicine and rehabilitation, and his colleagues found that TBI's cognitive effects may include language and communication difficulties, intellectual deficits, memory and learning deficits, and attentional deficits.[39]

General student characteristics. In this broad category, I address often-overlooked characteristics, including whether students believe they are impulsive, spacey (or daydream a lot), distractible, hyperactive, or depressed, and whether they tend to procrastinate. I ask about effective study habits, difficulty with organization or time, difficulty with concentration or focus, or any addictive habits. These questions get at characteristics that can be major impediments to successful learning in a typical North American academic environment requiring considerable focus, organization, and attention to detail. Students know themselves quite well, and they're surprisingly open about their habits, often readily admitting that they're easily distracted, are depressed, practice poor study habits, or have addictive behaviors such as smoking and abusing alcohol (research documents a connection between ADHD and addictive behaviors). I purposely don't commit to memory specific answers by individual students here, because I don't want to pre-judge students; I prefer to get to know them first. Then, if problems do arise, I can always refer back to this section of the questionnaire.

I also ask about any health issues that might impede success in the foreign-language sequence. There are all kinds of possibilities here (e.g., chronic fatigue syndrome) that I should know about. I also invite students to write about such issues in their weekly journals.

Finally, I ask students to describe their learning difficulties in general, and to explain any concerns they have. While some students demonstrate fine self-knowledge and know what they need to do to succeed, others are unsure about the precise nature of their learning difficulties. Some of my students who are eligible for accommodations (such as extended time for tests or a distraction-free environment) don't use them for fear of being viewed as less capable than other students; many want to see if they can do it on their own—the learning-disability stigma persists. A fairly high number of students say that they are seriously concerned because they have previously failed at learning a foreign language. So in the first few days and weeks of class, I seek to allay the fears and reduce the anxieties that many students bring into the classroom. As Mel Levine contends, too much anxiety can hinder a student's attention and memory.[40] Levine argues that students need healthy intellectual self-esteem, or "solid confidence in their own learning ability"; without it, kids who think they're not too bright keep on thinking that way. Students who have confidence in their intellectual abilities continue to have it. These kinds of self-perceptions often become self-fulfilling prophecies. Students who genuinely believe that they have intellectual ability are more likely to demonstrate it.[41]

The Joy of Learning

My fairly extensive new-student questionnaire helps me to serve my students, including those who carry low self-esteem because of previous learning difficulties. It also motivates me to continue learning about the intersection of foreign-language instruction and student learning difficulties.

I don't see the survey results merely as a tool for identifying student problems, however, because the survey also helps me get to know individual students as distinct persons with their own life stories and their own abilities waiting to be more fully tapped. The most learning-challenged students can be an amazing joy to teach and to learn from. They instruct me daily about life through their own experiences. As I document throughout this book, my at-risk, second-language learners represent a kind of human diversity that holds tremendous capacity for serving the whole of humanity.

4

Using Journals to Help
Students Learn How to Learn

Whenever I go abroad, I always keep a journal. I use it partly to help me remember the details of the journey, and partly as a place for me to write down thoughts and impressions—including why people of a culture act particular ways. A journal helps me sort through my experiences. Similarly I want my students to keep a journal of their journey through my modified foreign-language program. I want them to write down their impressions, wonder why we are studying and learning in particular ways, and sort through their own educational experiences.

I've discovered that journaling can contribute successfully to foreign-language learning among even some of the most at-risk students with significant home, school, and personal challenges. In this chapter, I first examine some of the helpful research on using student journals to improve instruction and learning. Second, I explain how journals work pedagogically in my own teaching. Third, I discuss the kinds of student reflection I hope to generate with two required sets of journal questions. Finally, I address common learning themes and the benefits of journaling for both student and teacher.

Exploring the Value of Student Journaling

A growing body of research addresses the value of journal writing as a means of reflecting on one's learning process, including learning a language.[1]

Professor of Education Anita Wenden, who taught in Taiwan and cofounded Earth and Peace Education Associates, believes that teachers should "try to gain an understanding of their learners' beliefs and acquired knowledge about language learning," and "aim to help language learners develop a more reflective and self-directed approach to learning their new language."[2] Scott G. Paris and Peter Winograd contend that student journals can help "effective teachers display both empathy and expertise; they guide students' learning with sensitivity. Classroom practices should allow teachers and students to discuss their thoughts and feelings about learning in order to promote metacognition and motivation."[3]

In tune with the research on metacognition I discussed in the previous chapter, journaling can heighten students' own understanding of why and how they learn. Writing about learner diaries as a tool to heighten meta-cognitive awareness, Carissa Young and Fong Yoke Sim—who have been teaching in a multicultural setting at the University of Singapore—suggest, "Positive feedback from teachers on diaries, to a certain extent, is an important motivating factor for students to be frank in their diary writing. Teachers' encouragement can carry students through difficult times." They add that "teachers' advice on learning skills enables students to think about the tasks that they are doing." Finally, they conclude that "teachers can gauge the intangible affective factors involved in their students' language learning by reading and responding to the students' diaries."[4]

Using Journals Well

I give students specific guidelines* for their journal submissions, such as typing and dating their entries, making sure each entry is a good solid paragraph, and putting them all into a folder when they hand them in. Students write two entries weekly, but I collect their journals every other week. About one-third of the journal entries are open ended, allowing students to write about whatever they like; the rest are directed questions. I tell students that I don't need to know about their personal lives, but that it could be helpful for both of us to know if they experience an issue in their life that impacts their learning. I indicate that the issue might be related to health, family, or learning difficulties. I encourage them to share the issue with me if they feel comfortable doing so. In other words, the issue should be affecting their learning and they should not have qualms about sharing the issue privately with me as their teacher.

Students turn in all their prior sets of entries with each new submission. This allows me to go back, if necessary, and look for themes, threads, consistencies, or apparent disparities.

Students should reflect specifically on the process of how they're learning French. Using nontechnical phrases such as "thinking about how your brain works" or "thinking about how you learn," I tell them that this metacognitive strategy will show us both how they are thinking, engaging course material, and responding to my instruction. Their entries should question and react, not provide answers. I inform students that I won't grade journal entries for grammar, mechanics, and neatness, but that they should check spelling and grammar before submitting entries. Spell-checking itself leads to interesting semantic issues—such as spelling the word "definitely" as "defiantly." Students assure me in writing that they "defiantly did all their homework."

Since many students have very poor handwriting, journal entries must be typed. Each entry must also be dated. The entire set (six full submissions of four entries each, per semester) needs to be kept in a loose-leaf folder so that submissions can be added throughout the semester. In order to help students stay on top of assignments, I ask them orally and in the syllabus* at the start of each semester to write journal due dates on their calendars.

Students may explain why they find aspects of French easy or difficult to learn—the "why" is important. Simply commenting on something is only the first step. I explain that a complete entry must address the "why" so that deep metacognitive reflection occurs. Students may journal about

- what they find enjoyable or unpleasant,
- what they find helpful or unhelpful,
- specific grammatical concepts they are struggling with,
- ideas that have helped them learn something better,
- what they think of a particular classroom activity or homework assignment,
- things they like or do not like,
- things that frustrate them,

- suggestions for things they would find helpful,
- questions about something discussed in class,
- concerns (e.g., about an upcoming test),
- their tutoring sessions,
- mnemonic devices they find particularly helpful,
- questions about why we are doing things in a given way, and/or
- cultural differences they find interesting.

Getting Feedback

Because immediate feedback is important for students to gain the most from their own journaling, I always grade the journals along with that night's homework and hand everything back the next day. I alert myself to the extra workload ahead of time by writing the dates on my personal calendar. Each journal submission is graded on a scale of √++, √+, √, √-, or √--, with a zero given if no submission is handed in, and a √++ if they have written thoughtful entries that show they have reflected deeply on various aspects of learning French. I use check marks rather than per-centage grades because students are writing about themselves and their experiences, and so it seems presumptuous to assign a number grade to such personal material that doesn't have right or wrong answers. Anything less than a √++ means the student hasn't met the goal of deep reflection on the journal topic. Usually this is due to a missing entry or a skimpy entry that needs more fleshing out. I allow students to resubmit those and I adjust their grade without penalty.

In my view, when students are sharing their beliefs and thoughts about themselves and their own learning process, they should be graded on whether they have done what is required (i.e., on the quality of the process of their thinking), not on their expressed thoughts, feelings, or opinions. For example, if they journal that they hate French and give a cogent reason, they still meet the writing requirements; I'll give a top grade of √++. Students won't be graded down for honesty, but honesty alone is insufficient. They need the freedom to state their true feelings, but, again, feelings alone are not adequate for full credit. So I will challenge students to explain why they find specific aspects of French distasteful.

I agree with Young and Sim that it's important to give students posi-tive, constructive feedback on their journals. Affect plays a major role in language learning, so learners need freedom to write about how they're feeling. Language-acquisition scholar Stephen D. Krashen argues that humans' "affective filter" is a "mental block" that prevents acquirers from using all of the "comprehensible input they receive for language acquisition." When learners' filters are "up," they might understand what they hear and read, but the input will not reach what Noam Chomsky calls the Language Acquisition Device. This occurs, says Krashen, when the acquirer is unmotivated, lacks self-confidence, is anxious, is defensive, or "considers the language class to be a place where his weakness will be revealed."[5] Many of my students are anxious, lack self-confidence, and worry that my classroom might indeed be a setting where they will be embarrassed for their weaknesses. When they start having negative feelings, their affective filters begin making them less receptive to learning. As a result, they might not be open on a given day to what they could learn. What if they look foolish? What if they answer incorrectly? What if they simply forget something they learned earlier and their mind goes blank? These kinds of "what ifs" can plague anxious language learners who lack adequate self-confidence. I need to keep affective filters in mind every time I interact with students in their journals too. I don't want any student to feel threatened, intimidated, or simply unappreciated because of something I wrote in their journal. Positive but honest feedback coaches journal writers just as it does sports players.

At the end of the semester, students turn in their entire journal. I reevaluate it and assign a numerical grade out of 100 percent. If students have received a √++ on all six submissions, they will get an "A" on journals. Within that "A," there will be a range from 95 to 100 percent, based on the excellence of the entries, as well as the timeliness and need for resubmissions. For each drop in grade (e.g., if there is one √+ and the rest of the grades are √++), I lower the letter grade one step (e.g., from an "A" to an "A–"). Journals count for 5 percent of the overall course grade.

Two Sample Lists of Directed Questions

1. *Talk about your last chapter test.*
   - i. How did you do on it?
   - ii. How did you study for it? Be specific.
     - a. What did you study? Vocab? Grammar? Listening? Other?

  b. Where did you study?

  c. For how long?

  d. Was it all in one sitting?

  e. Did you study alone? If you studied with someone else, with whom?

  f. What kind of environment do you need when you study for a test? Quiet place? Lighting? Food? Music?

iii. How much of the homework for that chapter did you hand in? How much of it did you correct for full credit?

iv. Did you correct your test for half the additional credit?

v. If so, what grade did you receive after correcting it?

I use the above set of questions* to get students to look carefully at their study habits and to see the correlations between their academic work and their test results. I often find that students wrongly attribute poor results to something that didn't actually cause the lower grade. These questions contain an implicit "why" question: "Why did your last test give the results that it did?" By coaching students in journals about asking the "why" question regarding their strong or weak performances, I am able to help them both identify and work on the real cause. So I genuinely want them to consider why they did well or poorly on a test. This becomes an important part of their ongoing learning, not just their journal writing.

For instance, a student journaled, *"I got a D– for my initial grade. It kind of surprised but not really. I knew that I didn't do very well on the test, I'm just glad that I didn't fail."* So far, so good. The student has expressed an honest, thoughtful answer. The student continued, *"I did my corrections, and got a higher grade (a C). I'm happy with it, just because I did so poorly on the test originally."* Here again, the student expresses feelings as well as affirms his or her own work toward a higher grade. The journal writer goes on,

> *I know that I did most of my corrections, but I seem to be having trouble with a couple simple things that I should know by now. I have a couple more days to correct the rest of them, so hopefully I can get around to that before they aren't taken any more. I'm sure there was a correlation between the two, because some of the parts on the test that I did poorly on were parts in the assignments that I messed up over and over.*

* see resource at www.foreignlanguagesforeveryone.com

Now it's clear that the student is really looking for an explanation for the poor grade. In fact, the student is acting like a researcher, examining a correlation in hopes of finding a possible cause and effect.

2. *Talk about the classroom environment.*
    i. Are you a spatially oriented person?
    ii. Do you learn/focus better staying in the same seat every day?
    iii. Would you like to have a new seat? Why or why not?
    iv. How would a new seat make you feel (e.g., More secure? Less secure?)?
    v. If you were the first person in the room and could sit anywhere you like, where would that be? Why?
    vi. With whom do you like to sit and why?
    vii. Do you think the same thing could be accomplished in another way?

I use the above questions* to get students thinking about how their spatial environment can affect their learning. Some students need to sit in the same seat every day to feel comfortable and to do quality work. Others seem to be able to sit anywhere from day to day. I also want students to reflect on their relational environment, namely, the interactions they use daily to develop relationships with classmates. The interactions might be fun—and might even relieve some of their classroom anxiety. But how do such relationships actually affect their learning?

I recall a student who never sat consistently in the same seat. In fact, the student often arrived at the last minute and seemed to grab whatever seat was vacant each day. Interestingly, this learner also never really connected with classmates—always seeming to be distant and remote. Moreover, the disconnected student rarely submitted homework, never handed in journals, was frequently absent or late for class, and was earning a failing grade. I encouraged the student to come to my office to talk about the situation.

When the student finally came to see me, we had a productive discussion. I learned that the student had begun the course with a self-described "bad attitude" about having to take it. I learned that the student never really took my course seriously and never felt vested in the class or classmates. I had the student look once again at the course contract. I asked my student to think about the contract and to consider re-signing it for the subsequent semester. Then a most amazing thing occurred. First, the student genuinely asked me to add to the contract a clause about the two of us meeting together regularly for accountability. Of course this helped reaffirm my commitment to the student too—not just the student's commitment to the course. During the following semester, the student seemed much more integrated into the class community. One sign of this was the fact that the student sat in the same seat more consistently, building relationships with classmates, especially those regularly seated nearby. The student successfully completed the foreign-language requirement.

Listening to the Major Topics in Student Journals

I've discovered at least ten important themes in student journals. These highlight both what concerns students and what they are learning. The issues themselves prove the value of student journals in teaching a second language to at-risk students. Topics include the following:

1. Self-awareness and self-efficacy (intellectual self-esteem, prior failure at foreign-language learning, perseverance at difficult tasks, personal characteristics)
2. Learning styles (auditory, visual, or kinesthetic)
3. Learning issues (such as organizational skills, sequencing skills, attention issues, sleep disorders)
4. Affective issues (such as anxiety and motivation)
5. Study habits and how such habits connect to learning results
6. Memory issues (difficulties and strategies, long- and short-term memory storage and retrieval)
7. Skills needed for effective foreign-language learning (including memorization, listening, imitation, willingness to make good guesses as well as make mistakes, using all the sensory modes, breaking things down into small, manageable chunks, analysis of patterns, and practice of patterns)
8. Value of journals
9. Cultural awareness
10. Other topics (e.g., tutoring sessions and the differences between the short January term and regular semesters)

Looking at Two Sample Journal Findings

In addition to the above-mentioned general themes, two common findings are mnemonic devices and the use of prepositions. Students are extremely inventive in coming up with memory strategies, one of which is mnemonic devices. Here are two examples:

- To remember that *samedi* means Saturday, one student came up with this memory aid: "My sister's boyfriend's name is Sam and they go out on Saturday night."
- Prepositions are particularly difficult to master in foreign languages. One student journaled, *"OK, these are really weird word games, and until now I really haven't had to resort to them in such desperation but the prepositions have done it. Sur ["on"] is one that is really hard for me to remember and the closest thing I could think of was that you pour syrup on your pancakes."*

Many people misuse prepositions. The other day on the radio I heard someone talk about how a heavy burden had been lifted "out of" his shoulders. What he meant to say, of course, was "from" or "off" his shoulders. I also heard someone say, "Come *at* the table" when the person meant, "Come *to* the table." Prepositions are often one of the last things language learners master well, both in foreign and native languages. You can often recognize a nonnative speaker of English by inaccurate preposition usage, especially in idioms. I've noticed that my students frequently say "on accident" instead of "by accident." Because many of them struggle with English grammar, they frequently use prepositions incorrectly. And since one's native language impacts foreign-language learning, I can predict from their preposition use in their English journals that they will also have errors in the target language.

Benefitting from Journals

Journaling benefits both my students and me. Journals help students better understand how their own minds work and how they learn best. Journals are a safe place to talk about their frustrations, concerns, comprehension gaps, learning strategies, and ideas and suggestions for how to improve.

Journals help students better understand the connections between how much learning they have achieved and the amount of studying and homework they have actually done. There is usually a fairly direct correlation. Students who don't do well on pencil-and-paper tests can still shine in journals—just like they can on a project.

There are also many benefits of journals for me as a teacher. They enable me to interact confidentially with my students, to encourage them when they feel discouraged or overwhelmed, to question their ideas, to challenge their assumptions, and to make suggestions. Journals allow me to examine my students' writing style in English—spelling patterns, letter reversals, and the like—to see the possible impact of their native-language skills on their foreign-language skills. I can also use student journals to ascertain how the class as a whole might be grasping or struggling with a new concept. Journals allow me personally to identify and address gaps in student learning—and how best to work more knowledgeably with individual students on their own learning strategies. Clearly the primary educational benefit of journals for teaching a foreign language to at-risk students is that they give me insight into how each individual learns best so that I can teach to their strengths and help them with any areas of weakness. This is nearly impossible to accomplish without journals. In fact, I don't know how it would be done except in one-on-one tutorials, which are far too expensive for schools to fund.

Improving Journaling

I continue to consider ways to improve my use of student journals. In addition to reviewing the scholarly literature now and again to see if there are items that I might include in future intake questionnaires, I watch for findings about the value of journaling, especially in foreign-language instruction. My list of personal research questions includes the following:

- How can journals be used even more effectively?
- Could students develop their own questions for journal entries?
- Can we assume that students act on their self-knowledge—even if they report in their journals that they are doing so?
- What are relevant privacy issues that teachers need to consider when using student journals?

- When is it appropriate for an instructor to encourage students to seek outside help for nonacademic issues that come up in student journals?
- Should the instructor and each student have a journal "contract"?
- Would it be worthwhile for some students to audio- or video-record some journal entries?
- How might I use my own students ethically as a kind of laboratory for researching the value of journaling—beyond the anecdotal information I collect in the process of using journals in my teaching?
- How could I actually measure the value of journals compared with that of other metacognitive tools?

Journals provide a rich source of potential learning for students and teachers. I strongly encourage you to consider how you might use them in your own teaching. Just as personal journals benefit many adults in their everyday lives, class journals help equip students to become self-teaching adults. I feel honored to participate in the journaling with my students. Reading about their learning victories is a joy that motivates me to continue serving at-risk students.

Reflecting on the Value of Journals

In this chapter, I examined the importance of journals in foreign-language teaching and learning for students with learning difficulties. Along with the use of intake questionnaires, journals help me better understand students' metacognition. They also help me determine how best to help students understand their own metacognition. The questionnaires provide a lot of information at the beginning of an academic term, whereas the journals equip me with ongoing research about each of my students' own views of their learning and my instruction. Journals even help me personalize my instruction for particular students. I've learned how valuable journaling is as an ongoing monitor of my own connection with students, and their connections with each other and themselves.

I adapt my metacognitive tools, including journaling, from year to year. For example, one student began her open-ended entries with intriguing questions to herself. I asked for permission to include some of them in my required questions for students. Students often say they run out of things to talk about, so they're grateful to have required questions, especially toward the end of the year. Students generally possess fairly good self-knowledge, even if they aren't always able to articulate it clearly or act on that knowledge in concrete and meaningful ways. I've been amazed at the wonderful ideas and suggestions my students have had over the years, and I'm grateful to them for what they have taught me, helping me to become a better teacher. My own educational journal, some of which I've essentially presented in this book, has been a journey toward greater self-knowledge and better teaching.

5

Teaching Directly and Explicitly to Maximize Student Learning

S ome years ago, a student asked me if there was a way to hear vocabulary words while studying at home. Back then, I couldn't figure out an efficient way to accomplish that worthwhile project. Now I record all vocabulary words for each chapter and post MP3 files* on our school's password-protected website. This enables students to listen to them online or download them to their portable devices, since nearly every student has a device that plays such files anywhere.

After I started recording vocabulary, I read a student journal entry that began, *"I have not been listening to the words online for one major reason."* Maybe this was a student without a computer? Maybe the student didn't like the recordings? The journal continued, *"When starting this class I listened to the words on a daily basis but was finding that listening to them was not benefitting me and was only hurting me."* Oh, no! What was I doing? What was happening with this student? But the journal added, *"I say this because I am a very visual learner, so what I would do is memorize a word and spell it how I saw it and pronounced it. Then when I would listen to the words online I would become very confused because the words were being pronounced differently than I had already learned them."*

In other words, this student was actually using my recordings to confuse herself! So much for the automatic benefits of new educational technologies. Actually that journal entry is particularly interesting with respect to how new foreign-language learners sometimes get mixed up

---

* see resource at www.foreignlanguagesforeveryone.com   91

about how to study and learn. I wrote to this student in the journal margin, "Unfortunately that means you are learning them wrong. I would suggest you start by listening to them and pronouncing them, and then learning how to spell them. What's happening is that you are using your English pronunciation system for French, and that can't be done."

In this chapter, I discuss the importance of direct and explicit instruction as a way of helping struggling students. Many foreign-language learners with learning difficulties need to know exactly *how* to learn—even how to teach themselves as they study. Because they do much better when instruction is very direct and explicit, I explain how to provide them with a pedagogical approach that suits their own learning needs. Since the concept of direct instruction has been discussed beneficially over the years, I first review the basic research. Then I look at the following six areas:

1. Phonology/orthography—including related morphology/semantics and syntax
2. Relating foreign-language patterns back to English equivalents
3. Inductive vs. deductive teaching and learning
4. Mnemonic devices, acronyms, chants, and spelling tips
5. Vocabulary lists and study hints
6. Technology to enhance learning

Understanding Direct and Explicit Instruction

The communicative approach, which has dominated foreign-language instruction for the last several decades, focuses on bridging a communication gap. It assumes that, with enough target-language modeling, students will begin to internalize the pronunciation, structures, and meaning. For struggling students, this isn't a hospitable approach, however, because it causes them to become very frustrated. They don't pick up by osmosis the structures they need in order to communicate. They need to be shown explicitly and directly exactly what they need to know.

There is plenty of helpful literature on the concept of direct and explicit instruction.[1] Particularly useful are Peter Winograd and Victoria Chou Hare's six characteristics of direct instruction: (1) structuring the learning in terms of clear academic goals broken down for maximal content coverage into manageable steps, (2) brisk pacing and selection of sequenced, structured materials, (3) providing detailed, redundant instructions and explanations with sufficient examples, (4) asking many questions and offering numerous overt active practice opportunities, (5) giving immediate, academically focused feedback and correction, especially when new material is being learned, and (6) active monitoring of student progress.[2] I've benefitted from weaving these into my methodology, as I explain in other chapters.

Richard L. Sparks and Leonore Ganschow, two of the leading researchers in foreign-language learning and learning disabilities, have long written about the importance of direct and explicit instruction for struggling students. Already in 1991, they and their colleagues discussed college students who struggled with foreign-language learning—many of whom didn't discover their difficulty until they had to meet a college foreign-language requirement. These researchers confirmed that there are young students with latent difficulties with the phonological and syntactic aspects of their native language which have gone unnoticed or for which the students have been able to compensate over their years of schooling. When confronted with a new linguistic symbol system—with new sounds, letter combinations, and syntactic structures—these students' basic difficulties reemerge and the language learners are "thrown back" into a situation similar to that which they encountered when originally learning to read and write their native language.[3]

Based on later research, Sparks and Ganschow still maintained that "for poor [foreign-language] learners, direct teaching of the phonological/orthographic [and grammatical rule] system is essential."[4] They concluded that the "natural" or "communicative" approach popular in foreign-language teaching in the 1980s and '90s simply didn't work well. Students with basic learning difficulties were wrongly expected to acquire a second language simply by listening to and conversing in the new language from the beginning. They wrote, "Our knowledge of how students classified as dyslexic learn to read, write and spell ran contrary to this assumption. We knew intuitively from the research on native language instruction that these students needed structure and systematic direct instruction in the rule systems of the foreign language."[5] What these scholars found with college students is undoubtedly true for students at lower levels as well. Many learners will perform more effectively in such an educational environment.

Teaching Phonology/Orthography Directly and Clearly

Please take a moment to pronounce these words aloud:

- through
- though
- ought
- rough
- cough

In each word, the "ough" is normally pronounced differently—not counting some regional variations. If you're a native speaker of English, you probably had no trouble distinguishing the relevant sounds. But a second-language learner is in for major confusion. The problem for them is that English isn't always pronounced the way it's written. This was my problem in first grade when as a Dutch speaker I first encountered the English word "Mrs." and pronounced it phonetically as "Murse" (rhyming with "nurse").

Phonology

Phonology is the correspondence between sounds (*phonemes*) and symbols (*graphemes*). This is an area that is often difficult for at-risk students, and the level of difficulty will vary by language, depending on how *transparent* a language is—that is, if, in the pronunciation of a language, "What you see is what you hear." The five English words listed above prove how utterly nontransparent English can be. French is another language lacking transparency. Spanish, German, Latin, and Italian, however, are much more transparent. If you're not familiar with the issue for second-language learners, do read a fascinating article by a literacy specialist about her frustrating attempts to master French.[6] There is also some interesting research on different pedagogical approaches for different languages.[7] German and Spanish "may require less focus on pronunciation and spelling because they are highly grapho-phonetic and have simpler sound-symbol patterns than English."[8] However, German and Spanish "may require more attention to grammar because they carry more inflectional endings on nouns, verbs, and adjectives than does English."[9]

Phonology is especially difficult for students with dyslexia. They're poor spellers in their native language and need direct instruction in learning which sounds go with which symbols. They need help learning when letters are "silent," such as the endings of many French verbs. Perhaps you remember learning to read English and being told that a silent "e" on some one-syllable words makes the vowel long rather than short (e.g., "kite" vs. "kit"). One French teacher calls these the "ninja letters" because they are there, but you can't hear them.[10]

Sparks and colleagues assert that sound and sound/symbol learning difficulties, especially in the native language, "play an important role in distinguishing good and poor language learners" and that foreign language instructors "should teach directly and explicitly the sound and sound/symbol (and grammar) systems" of a foreign language.[11] They published a helpful study on a model of instruction for at-risk learners that emphasizes direct instruction in the phonology/orthography of a foreign-language. Unlike communicative approaches, their "multisensory structured language" (MSL) approach focused on teaching the foreign language "in a direct fashion."[12]

I've pursued this kind of direct and explicit pedagogy for teaching sounds and symbols. I created a handout* that lists all the vowel sounds in French, gives their phonetic transcription (as found in a dictionary), provides the various spellings of each sound, and then provides examples of each one. I made a similar handout for French consonants and nasal vowels. At the beginning of the year, I spend considerable class time going over these direct-teaching sheets; students also work through them with their tutors. Students can refer back to these handouts throughout the year.

Because many students struggle with the pronunciation of words, I spend time repeating vocabulary words before the daily quiz. Students follow along visually, while repeating the given words or phrases after me. I listen carefully and correct them as necessary. While a few students grasp pronunciation quickly, I never assume that they'll pick it up on their own. When a word or phrase is particularly difficult, I break it down into smaller chunks and then reassemble it for them. For example, with the tricky but common word *aujourd'hui* ("today")—which sounds to my students like jumbled vowels—I'll say *au* (students repeat), *jour* (students repeat), *d'hui* (students repeat) and then repeat the entire word and have the students repeat it. I also explain the meanings of the smaller subsets of the word (i.e., *au* = "to the"; *jour* = "day"; *d'hui* = "of eight"—without pronouncing the *t* of the French word for "eight" (*huit*).[13] By breaking words down, students can see their constituent parts, and thus hopefully remember them better. Sometimes I start from the end of the word or phrase and work forward. When letters are silent, I often suggest students draw brackets around them. When a final consonant *is* pronounced, I suggest they underline it.

Students also work with their tutors on vocabulary pronunciation. At the start of each chapter of the course textbook, repeating new vocabulary is a significant portion of that week's tutoring session. While a couple of students every year develop excellent pronunciation, a much larger percentage never develops strong and authentic pronunciation because their auditory skills are just too weak. They simply don't *hear* the fine distinctions between sounds and thus have a hard time reproducing them. Many students continue to impose the English phonological system on French words; they just can't seem to switch. I use online video resources* that humorously demonstrate this to students.

As I mentioned at the beginning of the chapter, I audio-record French phrases for students to review online or download. A student journaled, *"I am finding online audio files to be a very helpful source. I found that hard when I took Spanish in high school to be at home doing the homework and not remembering how to pronounce the words. Having the audio files available like this is a very excellent way to help students in learning French."* Another student journaled, *"What really helps is going online and listening to the words first then writing the word out and at the same time saying it. This helps me memorize the spelling and then recognizing the pronunciation of the word."* I'm delighted when my students combine the multisensory elements of listening, speaking, and writing. It means they are learning.

Teaching Morphology/Semantics Directly and Clearly

Now try saying these multisyllable English words aloud:

- anthropological
- premeditation
- denominationalism
- photovoltaic
- antidisestablishmentarianism

*see resource at www.foreignlanguagesforeveryone.com

I know that the last one is a doozy, but it's also one of the longer words that many learners of English as a second language discover early on because it's playfully rumored to be the longest word in English dictionaries. In any case, you probably recognized some of the words immediately and didn't need to break them into segments of meaning. You also knew on which syllable the stress falls (e.g., premedi*ta*tion). Usage tells you automatically where the "invisible" accent mark is. But how did you do with the doozy? Would you know what these words *mean* if you couldn't separate the parts? The joys of English . . .

Morphology

Morphology is the breaking down of words or phrases into meaningful segments. Strong second-language learners quickly see how words can be segmented, but at-risk students can't do this very easily. To them, a long word is often just a long glob of letters, and impossible to pronounce. They need help seeing the segments and using the smaller parts within a word to form meaning. They also have difficulty combining segments whose meaning they *do* know and permuting the segments to create new words (e.g., taking "anthropo" and making the new word "anthropomorphism"). Morphology is thus directly connected to the *semantics* of language—to the meaning of words.[14]

I explicitly help my students break down individual words and short phrases into their constituent parts, such as their prefixes. With verbs, it is helpful to identify prefixes such as *re-* ("again") and *pré-* ("before"). Thus *revenir* means "to come back" and *prévenir* means "to come before" (i.e., "to warn"). *Remettre* means "to put back," while *recommencer* means "to begin again." The word *mademoiselle* ("Miss") can be broken down into *ma* and *demoiselle* to mean "my" and "young lady." Similarly the word *madame* means "my lady" and *monsieur* means "my gentleman." After a while, students begin to see patterns and learn to extend those to new segments and larger words built from the morphemes they already know. They become less "antilanguage," so to speak—"anti" is a good way to start getting the meaning of that doozy of a word. "Doozy" came from "duesie," which came from the name of the automobile in the 1920s and '30s—the Duesenberg.

It often helps to give students the literal meaning of a word or phrase. There are many examples—including words that students might use in English.[15] A phrase used often in English is *coup d'état*, which literally means "hit of state," but we would translate as "government overthrow." I point out that we pronounce it the way the French do. Thus the *p* of *coup* is silent, as is the second *t* in *état*. If students know the meaning of the smaller segments, they can then extend that to quickly understand that *les États-Unis* means "the States United," or "the United States"—they should also have an easier time figuring out that *prendre un coup de soleil* ("to get sunburned") literally means "to take a hit of sun." The well-known phrase *au revoir*, which means "good-bye," literally means "to the re-seeing" or "to the seeing again," in the sense of "until we see each other again." Knowing this means that they recognize the prefix *re* and know that *voir* means "to see."[16]

Being able to segment words into morphemes is important for knowing where the stress will fall in a word or phrase. Misplaced stress can lead to miscomprehension. If you heard me say that "I want to develOP [sounds like "devil up"] a plan for next week," would you know what I meant? In English, the stress falls on the middle syllable, but in French, stress generally falls on the final syllable. Thus, if you took a short phrase and extended it little by little, the stress would continue to fall at the end. Example:

- *Hen/RI!* (Henry!)
- *Hen/RI! Tu/as/un/bon/BON?* (Henry! Do you have a candy?)
- *Hen/RI! Tu/as/un/bon/bon/pour/MOI?* (Henry! Do you have a candy for me?)

Adding a kinesthetic element to this activity makes it even more effective. It helps students to *feel* each syllable and where the stress falls. Chapter 1 describes the use of rubber bands to help students develop a sense of word intonation patterns. As you can see, it is importANT to put the emPHAsis on the right sylLAble and not to wait until TOmorrow!

Teaching Syntax Directly and Clearly

Syntax is putting phrases together to form coherent sentences. Strong second-language learners quickly master the syntactical patterns of a new language, but at-risk learners need direct instruction in this area. They lack an intuitive sense for how nouns, verbs, and other parts of speech

* see resource at www.foreignlanguagesforeveryone.com

function in particular sentences. For example, some students struggle to realize that in the sentence "John goes home," the understood subject pronoun is "he." Similarly in the sentence "John and Mary go home," the understood subject is "they." If students don't realize this, they will have difficulty putting the correct ending on a verb.[17]

Some teachers use Madlibs as a fun way to help their students develop more grammatical sensitivity and better syntactical understanding.[18] These are sentences in which some elements are left blank and students must randomly insert a word that is a specific part of speech—such as a noun or a verb—into the blanks. For example: "The big _____ (give the name of an animal) who was at _____ (give the name of a place), _____ (give a past-tense verb) the only _____ (give a noun) very _____ (give an adverb)." One variation on the completed sentence might read as follows: "The big *robin* who was at *the restaurant squeezed* the only *basket-ball* very *slowly*." A number of such silly sentences can be strung together to form a strange, but perhaps memorable, story. Perhaps teachers who use the teaching-proficiency-through-reading-and-storytelling method (TPRS) could incorporate this idea into their instruction.

Earlier I mentioned that I recall as a little girl my immigrant father asking people on the phone, "Is it that you are going to be home tomorrow?" This seemed like awkward phrasing to me, but for him it was a way of avoiding the complicated inversion of subject and verb ("Are you going to be . . . ?"). Similarly the French have a valuable phrase to form questions: *Est-ce que* ("Is it that . . . ?"). I tell students the literal meaning, and as they begin to give replies to questions, I point out that the reverse of *Est-ce* ("Is it") is *C'est* ("It is").[19] When I later introduce question formation with inversion of subject and verb, my students realize how very useful this phrase is! As the course advances, the concept undergoes frequent repetition and spiraling to build more and more complex structures. I directly explain these inversions to students; I don't assume that they will automatically pick up such syntactical maneuvers.

Another example of direct instruction in syntax is the possessive form. Since *'s* (as in "Marie's book") doesn't exist in French, students have to rethink this phrase as "the book of Marie" in order to get the right phrasing. For strong second-language learners, this is a simple concept picked up intuitively, but it needs to be explained to students who don't make these connections automatically.

When French people say they're hungry or thirsty, they use the verb *avoir* ("to have"). This is true in German (*Hunger haben*) as well as in Spanish (*tener hambre*). So the phrase "I *am* hungry/thirsty" is expressed as "I *have* hunger/thirst" (*J'ai faim/soif*). This is another concept I teach directly and never assume my students will pick up automatically or extend it to new expressions, such as "I *have* heat" for "I *am* hot."

Relative pronouns *qui* ("who") and *que* ("which, that") are another concept that I teach very explicitly. The syntactical structure is similar in Spanish (where "who" is *quien* and "what" is *que*) and German (where "who" can be *der, die*, or *das* in the nominative case and has additional forms in the other cases, and "what" is *was*). I give students a simple rule of thumb: "If there is a more complicated, or maybe more formal or old-fashioned, way to say something in English, then that's how you'll say it in French!" For example, when translating the sentence "The book you see is old," students need to rethink it in English as "The book *that* you see is old," in order to translate it correctly. Or if the sentence is "The man you are talking to is old," students need to rephrase this into the more formal sentence "The man *to whom* you are talking is old." Some teachers give literal translations of subject/verb phrases that include a reflexive pronoun, since we don't use these the same way in English (e.g., French: *Je me lave les mains*; German: *Ich wasche mir die Hände*; Spanish: *Me lavo las manos*; which all mean: "I wash *to myself* the hands"). These examples demonstrate the learning benefit of seeing how foreign-language patterns relate back to English ones.

Relating Foreign-Language Patterns Back to English

One major advantage of relating foreign-language patterns back to similarities in English is that it helps students connect new knowledge to something they already know (even if they can't articulate a specific English grammatical rule for it). The examples I'll give are irregular verbs, cognates, false cognates, and translation of several major verb tenses, prepositions, and reflexive pronouns.

Irregular Verbs

How easily could you give me the principal parts of the verb "to swim" in the first person singular? "I _____ today. I _____ yesterday. I have _____ many times." Now do the same for the verb "to lie down." Very few native speakers of English can do these two verbs correctly. Bravo! if you said: "I swim today. I *swam* yesterday. I *have swum* many times." "I lie down today. I *lay* down yesterday. I *have lain* down many times."

Students are often frustrated with the many irregular verbs they need to learn in a foreign language, but I show them that we do similar things in English.* For instance, I ask them why we say, "I talk today; I talk*ed* yesterday; I *have* talk*ed* many times," but we don't say "I speak today; I speak*ed* yesterday; I *have* speak*ed* many times." Until they begin sorting out the differences, young children natively acquiring English internalize a rule about forming past tense by making all irregular verbs regular. We know that adding -*ed* is the predictable and regular way to form past tense in English, but there are many exceptions to this rule. Students need to be taught irregular verbs directly and explicitly with frequent review. It's especially helpful to teach them how to look for patterns and similarities among different irregular verbs. When my students and I put the "four big verbs" in French side by side, we quickly see that the third-person plural forms (*ils* and *elles*) all rhyme.

Cognates

I also spend class time on cognates, false cognates, closely connected words, and words borrowed directly from French into English. Once again, I give a rule of thumb: "If there's a fancier or more formal word choice in English, then that is likely the word used in French." An example is the French word *améliorer*, which means "to improve, to make better, to ameliorate." It's the last meaning that looks most like the French word and what I call "a five-dollar word to take to the coffee shop to impress your friends!" Similarly the French word *le visage* ("the face") is the equivalent of the old English word "visage," which today would probably only be found in poetry or in the King James Bible.

False Cognates

Many languages have false cognates, called *faux amis* ("false friends") in French. In Spanish, they're called *falsos amigos*; in German, they are *falsche Freunde*. These often lead to misinterpretation. For example, the phrase *passer un examen* doesn't mean "to *pass* an exam," but "to *take* an exam"—literally "to *pass through* an exam." Examples like this abound in every language. Some German examples are *fast* ("almost") and *also* ("thus"). A common Spanish example is *embarazada* ("pregnant"), which is sometimes mistakenly used when the speaker intends to say "embarrassed."[20]

There are also many words that are closely linked between French and English—probably due to similar origins in Latin. For example, the word *épaule* ("shoulder") is similar to the English word "epaulets," which refers to ornaments worn on the shoulders of a military uniform. There are also hundreds of words* that have been borrowed from French into English; they retain, as much as possible, their original French pronunciation.[21] I give the example of the word "ballet" and ask why we don't pronounce the "t" at the end of the word.[22] Other languages have similar words that we have brought into English but pronounce as in the native language, for example, *tortilla* ("tortilla") in Spanish or *Gesundheit* ("Bless you!" but literally "good health") in German.

This correlation between foreign languages and English can also be used to teach pronunciation rules, such as liaison between vowels and consonants and how these sound in different environments. For example, why do we say in English *vis-à-vis* ("vee-za-vee") and not "vis-à-vis" ("vi-sa-vis")? Consider how we pronounce the following words in English: *bon voyage, laissez-faire, joie de vivre, sous-chef, art nouveau, banal, croissant,* or *hors d'oeuvres.* Even in English, they sound French because we've retained the French phonology. Similarly we pronounce the *d* of the German *Gesundheit* as a *t* because that is how the Germans pronounce it. Likewise the *ll* of *tortilla*.[23]

Verb Tenses

I also teach very explicitly the differences and similarities in verb translations. In the present tense, the subject pronoun and verb form generally have three English translations, despite having only one form in French. For example, *je chante* is translated "I sing; I do sing; I am singing." Because that is true, students need to understand the converse—that when they want to say "I am singing" in French, there is only one possibility: *je chante.* They should not begin by figuring out how to say "I am," because the "am" part is basically empty of meaning. Students need to focus on the "I" and the "sing."[24] So I explain that to students before they start trying to use the various forms.

* see resource at www.foreignlanguagesforeveryone.com

Prepositions and Reflexive Pronouns

Prepositions and reflexive pronouns are additional areas where relating a foreign-language pattern back to its English equivalent can really help students. For example, the colloquial sentence "Who are you talking to?" needs to be permuted into the more formal "*To whom* are you talking?" in order to get the correct French equivalent. And the English sentence "We get up at seven every morning" needs to be reimagined as "We get *ourselves* up at seven every morning."

Teaching Inductively and Deductively

As I posit throughout this chapter, grammatical concepts need to be taught very explicitly to at-risk students. Although sometimes it is more effective to teach them *deductively* (i.e., to state the rule and then to give examples), at other times it's better to lead students from examples into the broader concept (i.e., to teach them *inductively*—from the Latin *in/ducere*—"to lead into"). As a general rule, I find that the deductive approach works best for new concepts which don't connect directly to something students have already learned, or for complicated concepts such as the subjunctive mood.

The inductive method works well by using "cognitive Velcro" to attach a new concept to something the students already know. For example, in teaching a new verb form, I sometimes give the students whiteboards and ask them write the infinitive form of the verb at the top along with its meaning (e.g., *sortir* = "to go out"). I then tell them what the verb stem is for the singular forms and what the endings are—the stem is *sor* and the endings then are *s, s, t*. Students need to write the forms: *sors, sors, sort*. Then I tell them that the stem for the plural forms is *sort*, and it takes regular plural endings. The students should then write: *sortons, sortez, sortent*. It helps to have students use one color for the verb stem and then trade markers with a neighbor to put the endings in a different color. While they're writing on their boards, I walk around the room, ensuring they're doing it correctly. Next the students translate the "I" form of the verb three ways into English: "I go out, I do go out, I am going out."[25] Once that is done, I ask students to repeat the verb forms aloud after me. All the while, each student is busy thinking, writing, and collaborating on how this new verb might work. After this activity, I hand out the daily gray sheet with a succinct explanation of the formation of the verb and examples of how it is used. We can now quickly review what students have just done "hands on." The sheet gives students something to take home and study.

By employing this kind of clear, direct, visual, and auditory teaching method, I've *led* students *into* a new concept in a natural way that involves all of them in the multimedia learning process. While the inductive method doesn't work well for all new concepts—such as those that are very complicated or have many exceptions—it works as a standard approach in most other situations.[26] As I teach new concepts, I always direct students to look for recurring patterns, since many at-risk students simply don't see such patterns on their own.

Considering Mnemonic Devices, Acronyms, Chants, and Spelling Tips

My son and his wife spent years in Africa working on international development and humanitarian aid. When they moved to Uganda, I decided it was time to learn the location of the countries of East Africa. Like most North Americans, I wasn't very familiar with the geography of that region. As a way to get three countries to stick in my brain, I came up with "USS" to represent Uganda, Sudan, and Somalia. Students are very good at coming up with *mnemonic devices* (memory aids) and other little tricks to help them remember things. They often explain these in their journals. With the students' permission, I share their best memory devices with the rest of the class. One student wrote about being able to remember *espérer* ("to hope") because it sounded like "despair," which is the opposite of "hope." Another student humorously remembered that the verb *s'asseoir* means "to sit" because it started with the letters "ass."

What does the word SCUBA stand for? How about AWOL or SNAFU? SCUBA stands for "self-contained underwater breathing apparatus," AWOL for "absent without leave," and SNAFU represents "situation normal all fouled up." An acronym is a single word composed of the first letters of the words of a compound term. Most French teachers know the famous "DR. and MRS. VANDER TRAMP" to remember which verbs are conjugated with *être* ("to be") as opposed to *avoir* ("to have"). Other languages elicit similar examples as generation upon generation of learners glean tips from teachers, books, websites, and educational recordings.[27]

Chants* and songs* can also help embed learning. When developing them, be sure to pick a catchy melody or rhythm that is already familiar.

One Spanish teacher uses the "Mexican Hat Dance" melody to teach the various forms of the verb *estar* ("to be").[28] The English song for the old TV show *The Addams Family* has been used to teach the days of the week in Spanish.[29]

I've developed a chanting melody* to help students remember an important grammatical rule in French. The *pas de* rule requires changes to various articles after a negative, such as *pas*. Language teachers are incredibly creative and could undoubtedly come up with similar chants to remember tricky rules. For instance, some German teachers have developed a song for remembering the prepositions that take the dative rather than the accusative. One high school teacher uses a song* with hand motions to help her students remember the meanings of prepositions, which can be notoriously difficult to master.[30]

Another teacher does a simple and elegant rhyme in Spanish with her students to help them memorize the demonstrative adjectives.[31] It goes like this: *este, ese, estos, esos* ("this, that, these, those"). She also likes to ask her students, "Do you want to be *estar*?," since that is one of the verbs that mean "to be."

Explicit spelling instruction helps students who tend to reverse vowel pairs, such as *ia* and *ai*.[32] If a word has a tricky spelling or is frequently misspelled by students, I'll point it out explicitly. I'll even ask students to circle or underline it on their vocabulary sheets. For example, the word *vaisselle* ("dishes") has two *s*'s and two *l*'s. I am constantly coming up with new tips, such as the fact that the direction of the accent on the French word *à* goes in the same direction as the tail of the letter.

When a word is particularly difficult, I might encourage students to write it out ten times (tactile mode). I might even suggest that they write it in large, printed letters, using the index finger of their nondominant hand to trace out its letters while repeating each letter as they trace. Maybe the brain pays more attention when the nondominant hand writes. This technique adds the sense of touch to the modes of seeing, hearing, and saying.

Teaching with Vocabulary Lists and Providing Study Hints

I strongly support the practice of giving students vocabulary lists for each chapter with columns in French and English.* For me, this is one more aspect of direct and explicit instruction. Students need to know which words they're required to master and to see them clearly laid out. The words must be spelled correctly. If students made up their own lists, they (especially dyslexic students) would invariably introduce numerous errors, resulting in some students studying misspelled words. Believing strongly in the value of using the tactile mode to embed meaning, I've considered asking students to write their own vocabulary lists, but decided students must have complete, accurate lists. They might not take the time to write out the words; some would have difficulty getting them all in the correct form. Vocabulary lists also allow me to give literal meanings of words/phrases. There is a strand of thinking in foreign-language pedagogy that advocates using no English at all when learning vocabulary. Pictures are often used for nouns. My textbook does some of that, but I find the pictures too ambiguous. For example, the picture for the phrase *une rue* ("a street") shows a building on the corner of a street with a young man riding a bike past it. So is it a picture of a store, a corner, or maybe a boy on a bike?

At the beginning of the year, I give students several handouts*:

1. Suggestions for Studying the Vocabulary Words
2. Characteristics of Good Language Learners
3. Study Hints for Learning a Second Language

During the first of week of class, I demonstrate a successful way to study the spelling and meaning of vocabulary. I tell students in the homework instructions to be sure to listen to the pronunciation of words online so that they hear the words. I show them how to begin by studying from French to English, and then doing the reverse. I suggest they put a check mark in front of words they couldn't remember and then go over those again. If they still don't remember, they put a second check mark in front. Then they go back over the words with a check mark until they can cross off the check mark—once for each check mark. They repeat this process until they have mastered all the words. If spelling is difficult, I encourage them to write out the word on a separate piece of paper rather than just look at it. Then when it's time to study for a test or the final exam, students immediately know which are their difficult words—the ones with the most check marks—and they can focus on those.

Early in the year, I ask students to write a journal entry about the second and third handouts, giving their reactions to the study hints and

* see resource at www.foreignlanguagesforeveryone.com

explaining which of the characteristics of good language learners apply to them. One student stated, *"The study hints for this class have been helpful to me in many ways. I already have a good understanding of how to study, but new information never hurts."* The student explained, *"I am the kind of person that needs to write everything down in order to remember it. I cannot just read something and then know it by memory. I have to make flashcards or at least write it down a couple of times for it to stick in my brain."* Such students gain a fine understanding of how they learn. As my students' journals indicate, this kind of applied self-knowledge helps them in other courses as well.

Employing Technology to Enhance Learning

Students with learning disabilities often have access to assistive technology, including speech-to-text and text-to-speech software. Most of this technology is designed for English speakers, but it is being adapted for use in foreign-language classrooms. For instance, I explained earlier how I created audio files for pronunciation of vocabulary words and posted them to our school's intranet for students to listen to online or to download to their own mobile players. Another technological development is software to help students with vocabulary. Several of my students have discovered software programs that allow them to manipulate vocabulary words in different ways. The most popular program allows them to create their own flash cards. I happily send students Microsoft Word documents of vocabulary lists that they need to fill out the templates that create their flash cards for printing. I think the new digital devices such as touch-sensitive computer screens and multimedia interfaces have great potential for providing students with a tactile means of writing out words. Please send me your technological ideas and practices so I can share them with others on the book website.*

The Value of Explicit Instruction

Direct, explicit instruction is critically important for students struggling with second-language learning. I strongly believe that this approach is good not only for at-risk students but also for all foreign-language students. While some students seem to be able to learn a second or third language quickly through osmosis, many learners are not so naturally talented. As I described at the beginning of the chapter, at-risk learners can get into trouble quickly if teachers don't make it absolutely clear how the foreign language works. When I started recording and posting pronunciation audio files to help students, I quickly discovered through their journals that some students were not using the recordings because they had already created their own mistaken ways of determining and remembering how to pronounce words. I continue to discover through journals, observations, and conversations with students how critically important it is to explain to at-risk learners what they need to know and why they need to know it as they grow to enjoy using another language and discovering the ways of another culture.

6

Serving Students
with Best Practices

Years ago I presented a paper at the "Best Practices Conference for Foreign and Second Language Teachers" held at George Mason University in Fairfax, Virginia. The concept of "best practices" was relatively new at the time. Program planners chose the conference title because there were educators who were "doing remarkable things in their classrooms."[1] Even today, many such remarkable things never appear in textbooks or scholarly publications. Instead they often are passed along in trade books, on websites, and through such conferences.

The term "best practices" has come to mean proven methods that professionals deem worthy of adoption. In education, outstanding teachers stay on the lookout for them. They know that even one really solid practice can transform an otherwise average class session into a highly productive and personally rewarding one.

In this chapter, I discuss some of the best practices that I've developed for teaching a foreign language to struggling students. I could include in this chapter some of the practices from earlier chapters as well, but since this is a short trade book, I hope you'll read all of the chapters even if you turned first to this one in order to glean some immediately helpful tips for next week's lesson plans. Some of the ideas in this chapter have been part of my own teaching for years. Others I gleaned from the excellent research by professors Doris M. Downey and Lynn E. Snyder, who wrote a seminal article on curricular accommodations for students with learning disabilities.[2] I developed and refined a few of their ideas specifically for foreign-language instruction. I cover the following foreign language–related best practices: (1) frequent repetition and review, (2) attention to affective issues, (3) cooperative learning activities, (4) tutoring and small group sessions, (5) gradual movement from English to the target language, (6) adjusted pace and content, (7) constant confirmation of comprehension, (8) variety of activities, and (9) incorporation of culture.

Repeating and Reviewing Frequently

I have young twin grandsons who love to have their Oma—me—read the same books to them over and over again. They never seem to tire of such classic poetry as "Hand, hand, fingers, thumb; Dum ditty, dum ditty, dum, dum, dum." Their Oma sees and hears how this kind of repetition effectively embeds words, pictures, and rhythm into their little brains. I also witness firsthand how they delight in hearing the same words and phrases over and over again. Children seem to know intuitively what we adults tend to ignore—that repetition is both a key ingredient and pleasurable aspect of learning. This seems to be especially true for songs, which combine a musical element with lyrics and rhythm. The German theologian Martin Luther famously said that "whoever sings once prays twice." He recognized the strong affective component of singing, which somehow embeds language—even scripture—into humans' conscious and subconscious minds. The same is true for another type of persuasion—advertising commercial jingles. People can remember for decades the commercial jingles they acquired in their earliest years of watching television. Already at eleven months of age, my grandsons could recognize an alphabet song. Moreover, when I sang it to them, they could walk over to the musical toy that produced the song.

In order to firmly embed a foreign language, students need lots of repetition and review of vocabulary and grammatical concepts.[3] As new material is introduced, it's important to build on students' prior knowledge, and spiral the concepts upward. First, I'll explain how I review vocabulary words. Then I'll elucidate how I introduce and review grammatical concepts.

Reviewing Vocabulary: The Building Blocks of Language

All students need to spend time mastering the pronunciation and meaning of new vocabulary. But this is especially true for struggling students because many of them continue to impose their English pronunciation onto foreign-language words. They're uneasy with a foreign-language phonological system, which is necessarily different from English. The students who have dyslexia already experienced great difficulty mastering the English phonological system; now they have to learn an entirely new system. A student journaled, *"I think the problem I am having with listening is that when I memorized the words for the vocabulary test I memorized them pronouncing them in my head the way they are spelled. Then when I go to pronounce them I pronounce them wrong or I hear them wrong."* Then the student further explained, *"If I would memorize them the was they are supposed to be said that would help but then I would do bad on my every day vocabulary quizzes because I wouldn't be able to spell them."*

This student is unable to learn the words without pronouncing them using the English phonological system, but simultaneously unable to recognize them when they're spoken correctly using the French phonological system. That is precisely why frequent repetition is so crucial. Students have to learn the sounds and symbols of the new language in order to get to the point of pronouncing them automatically. Vocabulary words are the building blocks of language, so students must master them well in order to succeed. It is like learning the keys on a piano or the letters on a keyboard. Students need to learn words one at a time and then keep practicing them orally and aurally until they become automatic. In this sense, repetition is the mother of learning.

My students have two important opportunities to get regular review and practice with new vocabulary. One is the weekly one-on-one tutoring sessions, where students go over new vocabulary by repeating the words after their tutors. Once a student is more comfortable with word pronunciations, the tutor has the student pronounce the vocabulary words by themselves, correcting the student as necessary.

The other opportunity is choral repetition of words in class before each day's quiz. I say the words or phrases and students repeat them after me. On the first day of class I tell them to imitate me exactly—in intonation (up or down) and stress (where the accent falls on a word or phrase), as well as in the articulation of vowels and consonants, of course. I tell them I love it when I hear rolling *r*'s; I sometimes exaggerate these for fun with the students. Such choral rolling even helps them lose their inhibitions about saying strange words.

Daily quizzes require students to master the vocabulary—but only in small, manageable chunks. Students who have experienced prior foreign-language failure talk about being overwhelmed by the large amounts of vocabulary. They say that the words never remained in their brains for very long, presumably because there was more total volume of vocabulary than adequate repetition of specific vocabulary. Some of them, especially dyslexic students, find that vocabulary is extremely difficult to master. One student journaled, *"To learn vocabulary and spelling I need to write the word over and over again until it becomes ingrained in my head. Then I need to say the words out loud and think about how it could be used in a sentenced or what kind of visual image I could put with the word to remember it."* Another one wrote, *"The continual work exercise homework quizzes were what kept me on track."* Both sets of comments illustrate the importance of repeating the foreign language's building blocks over and over again.

Since I always administer the vocabulary quiz* at the start of class, many students do a quick word review right before class. Some write out the words five to ten times for practice. Students who do this seem to score the highest—although they might also be the students who spend more time studying the vocabulary since the last class session. Nevertheless, I think that by writing out the words (tactile mode) learners add a fourth mode (in addition to seeing, hearing, and saying during choral repetition) to embed the spelling.

Reviewing Grammatical Concepts

In my experience, students similarly need to repeat grammatical concepts as frequently as possible. Before I present something new, we always begin by reviewing together what we covered the day before. I want to engage the students first by eliciting from them what they remember about the prior day's lesson. I conduct the review visually by writing down the topic on a blank overhead. For example, I write, *Futur Immédiat* ("immediate future tense"). I then ask students to share anything they remember about this concept. I quickly write on the overhead whatever they come up with, making sure to include some examples so each of my recall cues is concrete. Most students—especially absentees from the previous session—write down these notes, which serve as a succinct distillation of the earlier lesson. Some students simply listen because they seem to learn better aurally. When students teach back to me and each other the previous day's lesson, they are mentally rehearsing what they learned—or perhaps what they briefly learned but then forgot. They comment in their journals about how helpful they find this regular reviewing. One student wrote, *"My concentration on the grammar lessons and the lesson reviews is crucial for how I score on tests and quizzes."*

Once we've reviewed the material from the previous day, we're now ready to build on it. I firmly believe in the notion of cognitive Velcro, where you attach a new concept and make it "stick" to what students already know. Building on prior knowledge, even if it is about the English language, makes the new knowledge adhere better.

Another thing that gets regular and frequent review is what I call "the four big verbs": *être* ("to be"), *avoir* ("to have"), *aller* ("to go"), and *faire* ("to make/do").[4] Three of these are the basis for other tenses and are the highest-frequency verbs. We review them in many different ways. A student favorite is to split the class into two groups and give the first person in each group a whiteboard, a marker, and an eraser. This person writes down the infinitive and its meaning. The object of the activity is to correctly conjugate the entire verb. When I give the signal, the contest begins. The first person writes down the "I" form of the verb and passes the board to the second person, who writes the "you" (familiar, singular) form. The third person writes the "he, she, it, one" form. The fourth person writes the "we" form; the fifth person writes the "you" (formal, plural) form; the last person writes the "they" (masculine and feminine) form of the verb. As the board gets passed from one student to the next, the students may commiserate with each and correct each other's work. The first team to conjugate the verb correctly with all pronouns wins.

Another way to review verbs is having students write them on the board or on an overhead transparency. They can do this in teams; the first team to get the verb right wins a point. As I mentioned earlier, I also keep a soft ball among my classroom supplies, using it sometimes to do a quick oral/aural review of the verbs. I announce the infinitive of the verb to be conjugated, and we all agree on what it means. The first student gives the "I" form and then throws the ball to another student, who gives the "you" (familiar, singular) form of the verb. So it goes as the students conjugate and toss the ball to each other until the verb is fully conjugated correctly. The same kind of activities can be done to review verb groups—such as the three main verbs groups in French: -*er* (e.g., *parler*—"to speak"), -*ir* (e.g., *finir*—"to finish"), and -*re* (e.g., *vendre*—"to sell").[5]

I use frequent repetition and review in my classroom as one of the best practices for foreign-language learning among at-risk students. Above, I've given some examples of language-related items that need to be reviewed regularly. Generally speaking, it pays to repeat and review the building blocks for learning a foreign language in order to embed them firmly in students' minds.

Attending to Affective Issues

My husband had to play a jury piece for his college course in organ. He memorized it thoroughly, but when he sat down before his professor, his mind suddenly went blank. When the professor gave him a copy of the music, he just as instantly remembered the piece so well that he played it flawlessly. When someone puts us on the spot, we may have similar experiences of forgetfulness—but then we suddenly recall it shortly thereafter. Anxiety affects human memory, especially when it comes to performance. In fact, all kinds of affective issues can affect learning.

Creating a Sense of Safety and Security

When one of my students arrived each day for class, she would always be unsure about where to sit. From what I could tell, this student hadn't really made any friends in the class. In fact, the student preferred to work alone, was highly anxious, and never volunteered to give answers—despite, as I determined later, probably knowing the answers better than any other students. She would talk to me only after class—and even then, very softly, fearfully, and with shaking hands. Remarkably this student had already taken three semesters of foreign language and now just needed to pass my sequence in order to graduate. Probably because of her performance anxiety, the student had failed foreign language previously. I was determined

*see resource at www.foreignlanguagesforeveryone.com

to create a safe space in which this anxious soul could be successful. In all other ways, this was a top-notch student who had a better understanding of the basics of French than almost any other student I've ever taught in my modified program. The student was unusual only in the extent of her anxiety. Most students experience some affective distress when learning another language with classmates, but for at-risk students this fear is often amplified.

To succeed in a foreign language, students must feel safe and secure. Research supports the importance of paying attention to affective issues in the classroom.[6] As Scott G. Paris and Peter Winograd concluded, a high level of student anxiety interferes with learning.[7] I've witnessed among my own students a strong correlation between anxiety and learning difficulty: anxious students have a much harder time mastering and retaining knowledge than those who are not. Scottish language-acquisition researchers Margaret Crombie and Hilary McColl encourage teachers to take steps to "remove stress and fear of failure" from the learning environment "in order to ensure that young people can allow themselves to learn from their mistakes with reassurance and appropriate guidance to consider their responses in a metacognitive way."[8]

All of my students are in my class because they struggle with foreign-language learning. Their sense of self-efficacy is very low. They're understandably very anxious about learning another language. Many have failed at it previously.

But there is plenty of hope. I've seen repeatedly that some pedagogies do reduce student stress and anxiety. One of my students wrote that the *"hands-on"* nature of my course made her *"a lot less anxious"* than did her previous classes. I want my students to understand that it's not just acceptable to make mistakes in my courses; in order to improve their proficiency in a foreign language, they *need* to make mistakes—mistakes are part of the learning and the fun of learning a second language. Mistakes will help them move forward from no proficiency to full fluency on the continuum of *interlanguage*—the language produced by nonnative speakers who are learning a second language. On the first day of class, I draw a picture of this continuum on the board to show students that learning another language is a process and doesn't just happen overnight. They see the continuum as I draw it and talk about it. I hope that image stays in their minds. Even more than that, I try to teach in ways that will reduce their anxiety as they move forward.

I also use student self-reflective journals to help them address affective issues related to their language-learning. These journals are an immediate and safe place for students to communicate their fears to themselves and to me—if they wish. The journals also give me an open avenue to write personal words of empathy and encouragement. For example, many students write in their early journals that their prior foreign language (usually Spanish) gets in the way of their French—the vocabulary items, the spelling, and the pronunciation. Students find it very reassuring when I tell them that this is a normal part of language learning and that it'll get better with time. If appropriate, I can quickly share confusion that I had along the way in my own second-language learning.

Reducing anxiety is the main reason why I want students to have the same teacher throughout the entire three-course sequence—someone who personally knows and supports them and who genuinely believes they can succeed. Research supports this practice.[9] Dorcas Francisco maintains that "special needs students can not only learn foreign languages, but they can also enjoy foreign languages if they have a teacher who believes in them and finds their education equally as important as that of other students."[10] Students are grateful that they don't have to adjust to a different instructor and style of teaching in each new second-language course. If schedules permit, students stay with the same tutor from one semester to the next, because they feel safe working with someone they know. Consistency of teacher and tutor is an essential component of the affective safety-and-security domain that helps students succeed.

Dealing with Test Anxiety

I pay close attention to other anxiety issues that might arise. Many students greatly fear taking tests and giving oral presentations in class. They write in their journals about how their brains sometimes freeze when they begin writing a test. Suddenly everything they've studied and know just slips out of their brains. During the course of the year, we discuss good test-taking strategies. I carefully monitor students' anxiety levels during tests. If I see a student struggling with a particular section, I might go over to that student, smile, put my hand on their shoulder if appropriate, and suggest taking a deep breath and then moving on to a different part and coming back to the section later. I also encourage students to trust the solid preparation they've done for the test—including all of the work we've done together in class. I want to remind them that they're not on their own. I'm cheering for them.

During tests I sometimes see students swing their legs back and forth, knock their knees together, or tap a pencil on the desk. This is often due to anxiety. For students with attention-deficit hyperactivity disorder (ADHD), such motion is a way to release their pent-up or nervous energy. As I mentioned earlier, I provide a magic box of "fiddle gadgets" that such students can manipulate during class—not during a test, of course, but testing times help me identify these physically anxious students.

Considering Additional Affective Challenges

At-risk students are likely to bring a variety of affective challenges into the classroom. These can include personal obsessions or compulsions (such as needing perfect control over their environment or over a homework assignment—for some, to the point of rewriting an entire assignment so that it looks "nice and neat"). Some have low self-esteem and wonder whether they can actually succeed at learning a foreign language. Some tend to procrastinate and then get further and further behind, so that they struggle to catch up, or they give up entirely. In this section, I discuss some of these challenges in more detail.

OCD. A significant affective area I've observed among my students is obsessive-compulsive issues, including obsessive-compulsive disorder (OCD). Some of them have such carefully restrained and perfect handwriting (unlike the students with dysgraphia) that I sometimes wonder how much energy goes into that control. While some students are very relaxed (too relaxed perhaps, so that their affective filter is far *too* low), others need to be incredibly organized. The latter students immediately resonate with the highly structured aspects of the course, such as the daily homework sheets and my carefully delineated course syllabus,* which lists the dates of all tests, journal due dates, and the final exam. For organizationally challenged students, the structured aspects of the course give them the boundaries they need to succeed. So I teach to their strengths by being far more structure-minded than I used to. They might wonder if I have a bit of OCD—at least compared to some of their other teachers.

Need for personal space. Some students find it hard to be in close proximity to other students during class; they need their personal space. One meticulously dressed student was bothered by classmates' body odor! Another student journaled, *"I'm more comfortable sitting behind rather than in front of people, just because then my anxieties don't flare as much. There is just something about people having to look past me that just eats at me funny."* Students are usually aware of their own OCD behavior, and several have written amazingly long and detailed journal entries about this aspect of their personalities. One wrote, *"Studying for the test tomorrow is getting me really nervous. I know, I know. I am always worrying about things, especially the tests."*

Procrastination. My students also become more aware and honest about procrastination. When I first began teaching the sequence for at-risk learners, I allowed assignments to be handed in late without penalty. I was trying to be generous and understanding. I recognized that sometimes students are overwhelmed with other homework. So my motto was "better late than never." I quickly dropped that motto as I learned that I was hindering students' own academic development. The more generous I became with late submissions, the later the submissions. Some students couldn't handle my grace; they just fell hopelessly behind. I learned that being firm was in their best interest. They need fair but precise boundaries that will extend some grace to them, but also penalize them if they get too far out of bounds. I developed a system of "grace slips,"* which has worked very well. At the start of each semester students are given twelve such slips. They may attach one slip for each day an assignment is late. But they get only twelve. After using up that dozen, they are out of grace.

Recovering from Fear and Failure

Many students have poor self-esteem and see themselves as being incapable of learning a foreign language. One student journaled insightfully, *"I have found myself not only following along with the overhead and the lecture, but also actually understanding and remembering the concepts."* The student explained,

> To me, this is thing incredible, because on a normal basis, I rarely find myself feeling as though I have benefited from the massive amount of time,

* see resource at www.foreignlanguagesforeveryone.com

energy, and work that I have so diligently put into the class. To actually be able to feel confident enough in myself and my abilities to raise my hand in class and answer a question, is thing I have rarely ever experienced in my entire academic education.

Then the student offered the most affirming words: *"Therefore, to be able to do that, and actually answer correctly, has been a giant success for me, in and of itself."* Such words affirmed the student and affirmed me. This is the kind of journal entry that shows me how important the affective dimensions of second-language instruction really are, particularly for students with learning difficulties.

Another student wrote, *"I have learned that I am capable of learning a foreign language, I do not need to just barely squeak by and pass with extra credit, I can learn it and really learn it. This class so far has helped me feel like I am truly accomplishing learning foreign language; though I still have struggles I am doing it."* I am so grateful that a student like this was able to gain life-serving self-confidence.

One of my students journaled about the difference between an earlier second-language experience and the approach we take in my courses: *"When I took the other language course, it moved at a much faster pace, but ultimately in the end frustration took over and my learning curve came to a plateau."* Then the student directly addressed the affective issues: *"I was always worried about my grade and that's when I finally gave up. In the end, what matters most is how much you actually learned. I believe that everyone learns differently. This is especially true for languages. I also believe this to be true for math courses. I am grateful for this course."* Worry. Fear. Performance anxiety. These are important affective issues among my students.

Throughout the year, I give students lots of positive affirmation, acknowledging their individual strengths and gifts, and encouraging them to build on those. For example, I once had a student who took basic English composition three times before successfully completing this graduation requirement. Despite poor spelling, handwriting, and syntax, the student had impressive higher-order thinking skills. In fact, the student did remarkably fine movie reviews for culture points as well as an excellent final PowerPoint presentation when this technology was still relatively rare.

When my students achieve academic victories, they are genuinely grateful—and so am I. They live with failure nearby and so look for signs of victory. One of my students who had a particularly negative foreign-language experience prior to my course wrote, *"Throughout my previous French class, I experienced crying in the bathroom after I would receive a test back and being embarrassed about saying dialogues in front of class. . . ."* That kind of powerfully emotional experience isn't uncommon. But as our class began developing, the student gained self-confidence. The student journaled, *"Things are starting to make me think different after just a few short weeks in this class. The French language isn't some mystery that every-one understood but me. I too, can conquer the nasal vowels and phlegmy 'r.' Aww . . . the sound of victory!"*

Viewing my students positively and hopefully is essential in my pedagogical approach. I look at what they can learn, not what they can't learn. I genuinely want students to be able to proudly show me what they can do instead of what they can't do. That is why I sometimes include an extra-credit point on vocabulary quizzes—simply to reward students who can come up with something additional, who might even come up with another way to write or say something.

Since most of my students come into my class with great trepidation, I know that one of my most important objectives at the beginning of the year must be to calm their fears and worries. So right from the beginning we meet in a small classroom where students can sit in a semicircle in order to get a sense that we're in the experience together. We're going to cooperate, not compete. I devised the next two best practices—cooperative learning activities, on the one hand, and small-group and tutoring sessions, on the other—specifically to address students' affective issues.

Promoting Cooperative Learning Activities

Students with deep anxiety do best in a classroom environment with con-siderable cooperation among students, partly because cooperative learning simply appears to be more effective.[11] Spanish professor Jonathan Arries of Old Dominion University found that "students who were shy about speaking in class benefitted tremendously from brief pair-work activities."[12]

Moving from Fear to Freedom

Because many students approach foreign-language classes anxiously, I've devised numerous cooperative learning activities to help allay their concerns. Many of my students are frightened of being called on in class. For some, this is true in all their classes, while for others such fear stems primarily from a prior foreign-language class in which they had severely negative experiences. Some students have told me about having anxiety attacks in previous foreign-language classes. They were so deathly afraid of being called on that they could barely breathe. Since they were often totally lost, they were petrified about giving a wrong answer that would make them look "dumb" in front of their peers.

One student journaled, "*. . . too afraid—too afraid to sounds stupid, too afraid to speak louder, too afraid to even attempt it the way I believe it to be because in my head, I have already guaranteed myself that I am or will be incorrect. I hate the pressure. I hate the whole class looking at me. I hate feeling stupid.*" I wrote back, "You need to make errors to succeed in foreign-language learning!! Try to be little easier on yourself, OK? There's no way you can have mastered the entire pronunciation system of French in 2 weeks! It will get better and better with time." To the idea that the whole class was looking, I responded, "I doubt that they are. They probably feel like you!" One can feel that student's fears just by reading the journal entry.

Another student wrote, "*In past language courses, I have experienced intimidating situations where the teacher singles out one person to speak in front of the rest of the class. Having trouble with foreign languages, this 'singling out' is hard for me because I generally do not like to be the center of attention.*" Again, the student's fears about being called on are palpable. But this same student continued, "*This class was a pleasant surprise because I am not intimidated by the students or the teacher. I feel as though I will be able to learn without having to worry about looking stupid.*" This is why I rarely call on individual students.

Using Cooperative Learning Techniques

In a traditional classroom setting, peppering individual students with questions, one after another, was a very effective learning technique for me. I didn't think twice about it, although I admit to having the luxury of teaching many fine students with solid academic backgrounds. But at-risk students who are highly anxious about being called on would probably freeze up in such rapid-fire questioning. They are not able to concentrate when they fear being put on the spot.

Questions to the whole class. When I throw out a question, I invite voluntary responses from anyone who would like to venture a reply. I give them plenty of time to think about what it means and how to formulate a reply. Then I encourage students to answer with a group response. I slowly repeat with the students the beginnings of an answer, encouraging the entire group to come up with something. For example, if I asked, "How old are you?," I'd expect students to respond, "I am _____ years old," filling in the blank with their own age. When doing these quick conversation activities, I sometimes put up an overhead transparency containing the questions, uncovering them one at a time to give some visual reinforcement to the students who are having difficulty understanding each question and formulating an answer.

Working in pairs. Another technique I employ is putting a list of conversation questions on an overhead transparency and asking students to work in pairs to pose them to each other. Meanwhile, I circulate through the room to confirm comprehension and to offer help if needed. Many students find it exceedingly difficult to hear a question and give a succinct answer. They first need to painstakingly decode the question, then slowly and deliberately formulate an answer. So I don't rush them.

Cooperative review activity. Sometimes I use a cooperative review activity that starts with giving each student a whiteboard, pen, and eraser. While I circulate among them, students work on their own to conjugate a verb, for example. They then compare their work with that of a partner, discuss differences, and decide on the best formulation of the given verb. When they're done, they hold up their boards for me to check.

Community and cooperation. One teacher has experimented with dividing her classes into *barrios* ("districts" or "neighborhoods") and giving each *barrio* of four students the choice of working for an A individually or as a group.[13] The idea of cooperation and community in the classroom intrigues me, partly because I am convinced that such a spirit is key to how students feel about being in a particular class. If pairings and other cooperative ventures can reduce student anxieties—and I think they can—I am all for them. In his wonderful book *The Courage to Teach*, Parker J. Palmer explores "the kind of community that teaching and learning require" and

* see resource at www.foreignlanguagesforeveryone.com

contends that "good teaching is always and essentially communal." He says that "different teachers with different gifts create community in surprisingly diverse ways, using widely divergent methods." Palmer adds, "Like teaching itself, creating educational community can never be reduced to technique. It emerges from a principle that can express itself in endless varieties, depending on the identity and integrity of the teacher."[14]

For me, this kind of classroom community experience is so important that I use it to explain my attendance policy to my students. I explain that daily attendance is mandatory—and not simply because students need to be present and actively participating in class every day for their own learning. Students are members of a learning community. They have both the responsibility and the joy to serve each other as they learn together. When one student is absent, it isn't just this student who misses out, but the entire class misses out on that student's unique contributions to the group.

Discovering More Benefits from Cooperative Learning

Many of my students naturally form bonds when they work together in class or outside of class. Every year some of the unlikeliest friendships develop between students who give each other mutual support. I'm repeatedly amazed at the resulting matches. What I considered a rather unlikely pairing turns out to be a delightful surprise. One pair included a technical wizard who could fix anything, figure out any sound system, and always be counted on to help with classroom technology. This was my dirt-under-the-fingernails student. The other serious, dutiful student did the homework carefully every night, always arrived on time, and was good at "working" my program. The latter had less innate language learning ability, but worked hard to achieve success. When they first sat and then started studying together, I thought to myself: "Oh, wow! How is this going to work out?!" The two of them held each other accountable by helping each other remember deadlines and generally being there for each other. They both successfully completed their foreign-language requirement. These pairings challenge common cultural stereotypes.

Working with Tutors and Small Groups

Tutoring is essential in my modified foreign-language sequence. During fall and spring semesters, students are required to meet one-on-one with a tutor in weekly, thirty-minute sessions. This is a safe place for them to learn. Tutoring activities are designed to reinforce classroom work, focusing on pronunciation, speaking, and other activities. Students may also schedule extra tutor time for additional help.

Selecting, Training, and Using Tutors and Small Group Leaders

I work hard to find good tutors among advanced French majors. I prefer to hire tutors who can continue the work both semesters; even longer is ideal. I look for tutors who are sensitive to the learning needs of struggling students and who will interact with students in a relaxed and resourceful manner. At the start of the year, I talk with the tutors about the nature of at-risk students and how to set realistic expectations. I ask them to read an article that nicely explains the difficulties at-risk students experience in the foreign-language classroom.[15] I also give them a list of common characteristics of at-risk students.[16]

For all tutoring sessions, I prepare careful, written instructions* so that tutors know exactly what they are to do—and how they should do it. I also include a time line so that the tutors know how to allocate their time. Each session includes practicing vocabulary pronunciation along with other activities to reinforce learning.

During our three-week intensive January term, my students meet for one hour every afternoon in groups of six to seven with a small group leader who ideally is a semester tutor familiar with the students' specific struggles. Sometimes the tutor is an upper-level French major to whom I give some advanced training. This session follows and reinforces the three-hour morning session. I look for successful majors who have a heart for at-risk students, are creative and flexible, can keep sessions lively and interesting, and can follow the lesson plan I prepare for them while adapting it as needed.

Starting with English and Gradually Moving toward the Target Language

Most contemporary foreign-language pedagogy recommends that teachers use the target language from day one. According to my experience, however, this isn't usually the best approach for at-risk students. I agree

* see resource at www.foreignlanguagesforeveryone.com

with Downey and Snyder's "hybrid approach," which includes teaching in English and the target language.[17]

Many of my students have auditory processing difficulties, such as slow speed and memory. Many also have weaknesses in putting together a sound and a symbol (phonology). Therefore, I gradually introduce the use of target language for classroom directives. In my view, these learners first need to feel comfortable in the class. So I use English to help them feel relaxed from the start. If they're too anxious, everything will go over their heads. I gradually use more and more target language. For example, once students have learned numbers up to one hundred, I give them textbook directions in French. Many other routine instructions that occur daily in class can also be done in the target language. But if I start teaching most lessons in French, I will quickly lose, frustrate, and even worry most of them. Moreover, most of my students have enough difficulty following and understanding the concepts in English. I always give French examples, however, both so they hear the sounds and so that some of the students can begin picking up the language that I use for them. All of the students need to hear as much French as possible, but it has to be at a level that is appropriate for them so they understand enough of it that they don't feel overwhelmed.

Adjusting Pace and Content

While most of the class materials I use are the same ones employed in traditional courses and in the accelerated sequence, I adjust the pace and edit the content to meet my students' learning needs. I agree with Downey and Snyder that texts are often poorly designed or try to cover too much material, that we have to prioritize content and recognize the appropriate pace for our own students to master concepts, and that we may need to emphasize high-frequency items.[18] These are vocabulary items or grammatical concepts used repeatedly when speaking a foreign language. For example, students need to have mastery over the verbs "to go," "to have," and "to be," because they are used all the time. By contrast, a verb like "to swim" is used much less frequently.

When I ask students during their course-admission interview* to describe their struggles in prior foreign-language learning, many of them talk about the extremely fast pace of their previous classes and how they often fell behind. That problem is inevitable when at-risk students are put in the same courses with all other students and expected to learn exactly the same amounts in precisely the same schedules—and using the same pedagogies.

I set a steady pace that isn't quite as fast as in a regular classroom. The slower pacing provides extra time for daily repetition and review. Also, it offers more time for students with slow auditory processing and other learning difficulties to acquire a foreign language. I've also learned that I can use the extra time to give at-risk students the extra daily positive reinforcement that helps them stay on track and feel good about themselves and their work.

One traditional technique for quick reinforcement is doing an exercise from the textbook that orally practices a new grammatical concept. This technique doesn't provide my students with enough reinforcement. Many of my students simply aren't strong aural/oral learners. Doing such a purely oral exercise doesn't provide them with enough explanation or help. Instead, I assign these kinds of exercises for *written* homework, where the tactile mode can help embed the new concept or pattern that has just been taught. Then I can talk about the concept and practice it with students in class. The extra first two steps—written homework and in-class explanation for reinforcement—slow down the pace and reduce what I can cover.

I also adjust the course content, deleting or reducing those areas that are less important for gaining a basic working knowledge of the second language. I want to embed the most significant building blocks for the language. I agree with Peter Winograd and Victoria Chou Hare that the "selection of sequenced, structured materials" is an important part of direct teaching.[19] In my sequence, content is selected for its importance, linguistic usefulness, and degree of difficulty. For instance, the first year of the sequence I taught subjunctive right after the students had just learned all the major verb tenses. I quickly noticed, however, that this was too much for them. The students had a fairly good grasp of verb tenses, but when I added the complicated subjunctive, it even confused students about the verbs and tenses that they already knew. I no longer teach subjunctive, since it is something that we rarely use in English, and it can be largely avoided in French, especially for beginning learners. Students now have a much firmer grasp of verb tenses. I also carefully select vocabulary words rather than assigning every word in every text chapter. I put an asterisk in front of less important words, which students need only to be able to recognize.

Continually Confirming Comprehension

Throughout every class session, I vigilantly confirm student comprehension. Since students with attention issues get distracted easily, especially during discussion of difficult concepts, I constantly scan the students to see if they're with me. My visual and aural hypersensitivity to students' comprehension sometimes leads to my being so attuned that I become overly sensitive to classroom noises, whispers, or comments. I try to filter out the things that aren't germane, while remaining alert for those moments when I sense lack of comprehension. If I notice that students are fading out, I stop and ask them to stand up and stretch. Or I pass out some *bonbons* ("candies"). Or I simply change the routine a little. As I mentioned earlier, some instructors report positive results when students sit balanced on a big round ball during class.

Keeping students engaged. In short, I seek to keep everyone engaged. I've also noticed it's important, especially for learners with ADHD, to make sure that they have the appropriate books and materials with them—and even that the materials are open to the correct pages. Sometimes, if a homework assignment has been unusually difficult, we go over it together to consider frequently made errors. When I do this, I first put up a blank overhead transparency and write on the top of it the exercise and page number, saying them in the target language. Sometimes even after all of that auditory and visual reinforcement, a student might still ask where we are. Normally it's a student with ADHD who needs both some teacher patience and an extra nudge. There's a fine line between honestly meeting the needs of students with ADHD and allowing them to become carelessly unfocused. But even just the rolling eyes of other students help unfocused students realize that they need to focus on the directions.

Announcing transitions. I warn students in advance when I am going to transition to something new. Some of my students clearly need this declaration, so I sometimes ask them to fill in a blank, underline something, or put an asterisk by the new material to call it to their attention as clearly and practically as possible without sounding like a nag.

More on the* bonbons *technique. Let me elaborate on the *bonbons* technique—who wouldn't like to talk about candy? When I see students beginning to fade out, I get out my box of *bonbons* and pass it around as a way to help students ingest a little quick energy. I simply want to help them stay motivated and focused on the task at hand. Students will sometimes ask if they may have one. I never simply accede to the one-word request of "*Bonbons?*" Students must learn how to put their request into a complete sentence if they are going to enjoy one of the goodies. "*Je voudrais un bonbon, s'il vous plaît*" works splendidly—"I would like a candy, please." This teaches them how to ask courteously in the target language, and how to use the polite form of the word "please." Students *never* forget that word! And if there is one vocabulary item that will stick with them forever, it is undoubtedly *bonbons*.

Varying Activities

Many at-risk students have attention issues, such as short attention span or difficulty knowing what to attend to and how to attend to it. This is why it's important to include a wide variety of activities in every class period. I aim to keep them engaged as long as their attention holds out before moving on to something else, so I have to be somewhat flexible with my daily scheduling within each class period. I also change tasks frequently within short work periods. For teachers on block schedules, this would be particularly pertinent. It's especially important during my January term, which includes a ninety-minute morning session. It all sounds like common sense, but the not-so-obvious part of keeping attention is paying attention to the attention of the students. I also concur with Mel Levine that during longer periods, the students need "periodic mind breaks."[20] Essentially the same as what I earlier called "brain recesses," these mind breaks provide a several-minute period for students to let their minds recharge. One student journaled that the *bonbon* candies I offered in class provided a mental break for him. He was able to enjoy the candy without having to think about language for a couple of minutes.

 * see resource at www.foreignlanguagesforeveryone.com

My students pick up on this approach to holding their attention—and they appreciate it. One of my students journaled, *"I like how we don't have the same format everyday If we didn't mix up the whiteboards, culture, games, and all of that I would probably get bored and not pay attention."* Then the student explained that in Spanish class she used to get bored and stop paying attention. *"I got so far behind that I couldn't keep up anymore."* Another student wrote, *"I like that we move along and do different things. It helps me stay interested. I also love to write on the whiteboards."* The whiteboards are so easy to use but so appreciated by hands-on learners.

Hands-on activities. My students do lots of "hands-on" activities: partner work, listening activities, videos, music, and singing. As I indicated earlier, my students enjoy reviewing vocabulary by passing tangible objects* (e.g., plastic foods such as fruits and vegetables, or items of clothing) and reviewing verbs by throwing a soft ball. Sometimes I ask a few students to go to the blackboard. I always assign small groups of students in their seats to work along with and monitor the students working at the board—partly to keep them all on task, and partly so that the students at the board don't get too anxious.

A listening activity. Once every few weeks, we do a textbook listening activity that focuses on deriving meaning from an oral/aural text. First, we review the French questions being asked so that students know what to listen for. Students may jot them down on their half sheet of scratch paper. I always collect these after the activity to verify students' level of comprehension and to ensure that they're all actively participating in the listening practice. Answers can be written in French or in English, and there is no penalty for misspellings. We listen to the entire text once, and students try to answer as many questions as possible. After we listen to it a second time, I pause the CD at the salient points in the text to help students figure out the correct answer. Many of the students with auditory processing difficulties have a hard time breaking down the speech stream. Pausing the CD allows them to reflect on the last part of the spoken text that they just heard. They should be saying it over in their heads. If students look extremely puzzled, I'll sometimes repeat the last segment myself, slowly and carefully, to help them decode it. At times, we discuss listening strategies, such as jotting down phrases that are familiar. Students share how they figured out the meaning of a particular phrase, and I give additional ideas. Occasionally I let students see the actual text of what they're hearing. For the visual learners, this is extremely helpful, but I don't do this regularly because then it would no longer be a purely listening activity.

Videos. We also occasionally view video segments that accompany the textbook materials. In order to hold students accountable, I usually give them a worksheet to complete, although some students feel that it detracts from their focus on the actual video. I sometimes encourage students to center on a specific aspect of the video, such as looking at the speakers' lips as they speak.[21] We also examine cultural differences and similarities (e.g., shopping carts in stores and greetings at a family party).

Music. When was the last time you heard a song that you could sing along with even though you hadn't heard it for years? For me, this happens with the ever-popular Beatles songs that suddenly show up on the radio or on the speakers at a restaurant or department store. I'm still amazed at how much I remember of such tunes. I'm a singer and have loved music since my childhood. I had high hopes for incorporating music and singing into my classes, but unfortunately this hasn't worked out exactly how I had anticipated. Perhaps it is because many of my students have weak auditory skills—some of them seem to be completely tone deaf or have great difficulty singing on pitch. Maybe that's why many of them don't even enjoy singing. Yet I persist. We begin each week with some kind of song, often singing simple rounds. At the start of the year, I teach the students the French alphabet song,* as well as other children's songs,* such as "*Tête, épaules, genoux et pieds*" ("Head and shoulders, knees and toes"), when learning the parts of the body. Students are happy to do the motions along with me; this taps into the kinesthetic mode of learning. At this simple level, music works quite well, seemingly with little student embarrassment once they get used to the routine.

One childhood song that was very popular during my childhood is simply these lyrics, repeated over and over, often in rounds: "Row, row, row your boat, gently down the stream, Merrily, merrily, merrily, merrily,

* see resource at www.foreignlanguagesforeveryone.com

life is but a dream." One person begins the round and then a second and third person begin each on the second and third line—causing everyone to be singing through each other in a sort of random chaos. As the year progresses, I aim for the students to sing rounds *en canon de trois groupes* ("in canon with three groups")—something that is quite tricky for students who get easily distracted by what a neighboring group is singing.

Many teachers have successfully incorporated music or singing into teaching. One teacher has her students sing the days of the week in Spanish to the tune* of "Brother John."[22] Another instructor has developed a rhythmic singing activity in Spanish to the tune of "Boom Boom."[23] She has students write down a singular food or beverage item, a plural food or beverage item, a singular body part, and plural body parts. She then has the students practice the verb *gustar* ("to like") and its unusual syntactical construction with singular or plural nouns to give students the feel for how this verb works.[24] This teacher has also developed an activity in Spanish to the tune of "California Girls," popularized originally by the Beach Boys and more recently recorded by rap artists. These Spanish examples demonstrate teachers' resourceful use of rhythmic and musical activities to help students learn.

Incorporating Culture

The American Council on the Teaching of Foreign Languages (ACTFL)* has developed national standards for foreign-language education. ACTFL stresses the importance of helping students develop the "Five Cs," one of which is cultural competence. As ACTFL puts it, students should work on "gain[ing] knowledge and understanding of other cultures."[25] There are many solid reasons for weaving cultural learning throughout foreign-language courses.

For one thing, you can't really learn another language without understanding the culture within which it is embedded. Because understanding another culture is vital to comprehending its people, I heavily emphasize culture in my classes. I also conduct semiannual workshops for preservice teachers on how to incorporate culture into the foreign-language classroom.

While culture has often been seen a bit drearily as learning facts and figures (such as the names of mountains and rivers, the kinds of food people eat, etc.), I help my students dig more deeply. I concur with H. Ned

Seelye and others who view culture as what humans do and have learned. Seelye quit high school at the end of his junior year and hitchhiked to Mexico, only to discover that, because he knew neither the language nor the culture, he had no future there. Later he went on to become a highly accomplished professor of sociology, anthropology, and language. Seelye defines culture robustly as "knowledge and behavior patterns provided by differing traditions to enable their culture bearers to satisfy basic physical and psychological needs."[26] So much of culture is what makes life fun and meaningful for people. I want my students to develop cross-cultural awareness of how people live and what people find worth doing. In today's globalized world, gaining this kind of cultural intelligence should be an indispensable, lifelong skill. There are many other excellent resources for helping our students develop good intercultural skills.[27] Approximately 12 to 15 percent of my students' overall course grade is based on an understanding of francophone culture. In addition to a culture section on every chapter test, students are also required to do a "culture project" and to earn thirty points of "culture credit" during each semester—fifteen points during our January term.

Culture section on chapter tests. When presented in an interesting way, cultural differences can truly engage students, including at-risk learners. Moreover, even those who struggle with second-language learning can easily learn a lot about another culture. I include a culture section on each chapter test. The cultural section looks at more than factual knowledge. I engage students by asking them to give their thoughts on various aspects of the target culture. Of course, in order to provide their own perspective, they have to know the underlying differences. For example, I ask students to explain whether they would prefer eating with French or American dinner practices, or whether they would like to be educated in the French system or the American. In both cases, students need to be able to describe the differences in order to explain their own preferences.

Culture project. Culture projects consist of an oral presentation given to the class as well as a research paper submitted to me. During the fall semester, students choose some well-known place in Paris as a topic. During our

* see resource at www.foreignlanguagesforeveryone.com

short January term, they choose a geographical location in France. During the spring semester, students choose a famous French person, living or dead. Students are given specific guidelines* for these oral and written projects. I also provide a list of suggested topics. A student may suggest a topic in tune with a personal interest—such as in the case of a college tennis player who chose the Roland-Garros Stadium for a Paris project, and Rafael Nadal for the famous person.

Culture credits. Students can earn thirty points of culture credit* in many different ways. They can get fifteen points for viewing a francophone film* and writing a one-paragraph summary along with a one-paragraph reaction, including what they considered to be the theme or point of the film. The film must be in French, with English subtitles, so that the students hear authentic target language. Non-French movies dubbed into French (e.g., *The Lion King*) aren't allowed, since they are basically North American movies. I want students to learn something about the nature of French cinema and to get a sense of film as art as well as entertainment.

Students can also earn culture points by bringing in French food for the entire class to taste. If they make the food themselves, they get fifteen points per dish; buying the food earns them ten points per item. I have plenty of cookbooks for students to use; there are also many resources available on the Internet. I tell students that the following foods can't be used because they aren't culturally authentic: French fries, French vanilla ice cream, and French toast. It is amazing to see some of the food that students have prepared! One student created an elaborate *bûche de Noël* ("Yule log"*) just before Christmas. Students can also attend a French chapel for three points—or get five points for participating in and leading it. Each year the French pronunciation of at least one of my students is good enough for that student to read scripture aloud during French chapel. Students can also pitch other ideas to me. Prior to the devastation there in 2005, a student met this requirement by spending spring break in New Orleans—and not entirely in the French Quarter. Sometimes students visit nearby art exhibits or go to concerts. Whatever students choose (other than food), they need to hand in a written reflection on their experience. In addition, students may submit a newspaper or magazine article, cartoon, advertisement, or something from the Internet that uses a French phrase or talks about something going on in the francophone world. They receive one point of culture credit for each such item.

More recently, I've been directing students to specific library books on French culture.[28] Students must read sections of these preapproved books, write a summary of their reading, and compose their personal reactions. They may choose book sections that interest them the most. For instance, a business major might choose book sections on doing business in France. I'm so convinced of the value of understanding French culture that this book assignment is now required for all students during spring semester. One student journaled,

> *French is certainly not a cake walk, but it does give you the opportunity to have your cake and eat it too in the sense that, if you work hard, you will know French and you will get a good grade. I mentioned that journals were second in ease only to culture points, this is true. Culture points are probably the easiest A you can get. All it takes is going to meijer and picking up some French food a few times, or watching a couple of movies and writing them up, or going to a bunch of French chapels or any number of other things that have to do with French culture. They account for 5% of the final grade and couldn't take much less effort to do well with if they had to. Culture points are also helpful in the sense that often the class gets to sample a bit of French food, which is all ways a good thing. The other options either gets one to go to chapel (also a good thing) or they force one to sit through an hour and half of French dialogue. This latter example can be of particular value since it helps me recognize phrases that I should know but might not understand because of the speed with which they are spoken. This comes in exceedingly handy when the test rolls around and I have to do a listening section. Having heard more French dialogue through the film(s) prepares me well to attempt to get a handle on what the people on the listening section of the test are saying.*

From a virtual tour of the Louvre Museum in Paris, to the music of Spain, to the food of China, nowadays there are many outstanding online resources for cultural learning. By doing research on their own and presenting their findings to the class, students can enrich everyone's cultural understanding.

Best Practices and the Love of Language, Culture, and Teaching

I used to supervise student teachers in second-language classrooms of all kinds—Spanish, French, German, Latin—from kindergarten to twelfth grade. One of the joys of that work was discovering the best practices that so many fine teachers had successfully discovered and implemented because of their love of language, culture, and teaching. The cooperating teachers who were training my preservice teachers were outstanding educators who had discovered their own best practices worthy of emulation. I salute outstanding foreign-language teachers everywhere who are eager to develop their teaching practice. I hope that my suggestions in this chapter will generate a new wave of contributions from such creative educators.

7

Equipping Students to Learn Responsibly

One of my students wrote in a course journal,

I think that one of the best things I found through this class is the confidence of being "normal." Although I know I am somewhat normal (having my unique God-given traits), having learning disabilities puts one at a disadvantage in classes. Being able to actually understand and remember (sometimes, I still struggle with my memory problem), to be able to fix mistakes in order to fix it in my mind as well . . . it all makes me feel amazingly confident. For once in such a very long time, I feel like the grade I'm getting is actually representing my understanding and ability, my hard work and sacrifice for the class and subject!!

While homework and test corrections are a lot of work for me, they're an essential component of what makes my modified foreign-language sequence successful. It gives courage to students who struggle but work hard every day. Journal entries like that one document how my approach to grading serves students for life.

In solid education, students and faculty are both responsible for student learning. We teachers are responsible for choosing curricula and figuring out how to deliver them in ways that truly meets students' learning needs. We're accountable for creating the kind of instruction that will encourage and even inspire students to become self-teaching learners. In the end, however, it's up to the students to digest it and put it into practice. One of my colleagues says that we simply pitch the ball—the students have to hit it![1] To extend this metaphor a little further, we could say that students need to develop hand-eye coordination, timing, and a proper hitting stance. And they need to step into the batter's box with a helmet!

In this chapter, I examine various aspects of helping students take ownership of their learning. I consider organizational skills, homework, testing, grading, study aids, and standards. Along the way, I introduce the IK Correction Method* and IK Grace Slip Method*—two important pedagogical tools that take a bit more teacher time but demonstrate considerable benefit for at-risk students in second-language learning.

Of course, how much work students put into their own learning varies from student to student, depending on many tangibles and intangibles, from personality, initiative, and time limitations to past academic experience, especially if that experience has been primarily negative. In discussing how metacognition can promote academic learning, Scott G. Paris and Peter Winograd identify the importance of students' self-perceptions, which often lead learners to avoid a task rather than risk failing at it. They indicate that most students prefer avoiding a task if they perceive little real gain. Paris and Winograd add that student perceptions include their expected payoff, their expectations for success, and the amount of effort that they think is required to accomplish the task.[2]

Many at-risk students do work very hard, but all too frequently their grades don't reflect their efforts. They easily become discouraged. This is one of the reasons why I give credit for corrections to homework assignments and tests. I aim for students to learn from their mistakes and to improve their grades, but I also want my students learn to choose for themselves how to succeed at a task. That will not only help them improve their perceptions of themselves, but help them become better learners.

Teaching Organizational Skills

An essential part of encouraging students to become responsible for their own learning is ensuring that they stay organized and on top of homework and test corrections, as well as all the other papers that are handed out regularly. As I mentioned earlier, at the start of the year I require all

* see resource at www.foreignlanguagesforeveryone.com

students to get a three-ring binder with tab inserts. I then have them label the inserts in advance for the different kinds of handouts that I will be distributing throughout the term.

One student journaled, *"Organization in this class is really invaluable. Prof. K. insists on some measure of organization in the beginning of the semester by checking folders for dividers."* The student admitted that the practice *"seemed rather silly at first,"* but then added, *"I came to find out that when it comes test time and you need to look back at all the gray sheets and vocab and who knows how many other hand-outs then you end up very, very thankful that you keep everything neat and organized."* That alone is a marvelous testament to student learning, but this learning-challenged journal writer went even further into the advantages of the organizational system: *"I think that good organization in the folder also helps to better organize things in my brain and this too is very helpful around test time."* The final comment about brain organization documents how this student connected tangible and mental organization. It shows metacognition at work.

Students also need to devise a system that allows them to keep track of homework assignments that still need to be corrected. I give students an inexpensive folder with pockets in which they can keep the completely corrected assignments in the back pocket and the ones that still need work in the front.

Homework—Making and Correcting Errors

Foreign-language pedagogy rightly assumes that students must make errors in order to progress in their proficiency. Michigan State University Professor of Education Jere Brophy even asserts that teachers should see errors as "natural and useful parts of the learning process rather than as evidence of failure."[3] Professor Andrew D. Cohen of the Program in Second Language Studies at the University of Minnesota believes that "corrections are important and make a real contribution, but only when you are ready for them and can benefit from them. Otherwise they may simply have a discouraging effect on your self-concept as a target language learner."[4]

At-risk students easily become disheartened. I believe that corrections are vitally important for their success, so I structure the process of making corrections in such a way that students' self-concepts are *en*couraged, not *dis*couraged.

What do students think about my approach? One journaled, *"Having the ability to go back and see what mistakes you make regularly and then even having the incentive to correct them on the paper and thus make it more likely that I remember it the next time was a large part of what has helped me to do relatively well in this class."* Another learner wrote, *"As far as what is necessary to succeed . . . you need to work hard. In particular you need to work hard at getting all of your homework done and then corrected, this helps a lot, not just for the grade boost that correcting itself provides but also as practice for the test."*

Introducing the IK Correction Method

Peter Winograd and Victoria Chou Hare emphasize "offering numerous overt active practice opportunities" and "active monitoring of student progress" as a means for helping students succeed at foreign-language learning.[5] The system of homework corrections that I've developed—the IK Correction Method—resonates with their suggestions. First, I give students many practice opportunities. Second, when they practice the art of correcting their own work, I carefully monitor their individual progress.

As I discussed in chapter 2, for each chapter of the textbook, I write and distribute a packet of structured homework assignments,* carefully delineating daily tasks to avoid any student confusion about what's required. I also give specific instructions on how they can—and should—correct homework assignments. Ultimately, students must decide for themselves whether to take on this responsibility for their own learning, but I do see a strong correlation between homework corrections and language mastery.

As the academic year progresses, I assign a journal question that asks students whether they see any correlation between their corrections and their related test scores. One student wrote in response, *"On my chapter 8 test I initially got a 79.5 percent and that grade did not surprise me. When I was studying I believed that I knew the material better than I actually did. After making corrections on test I raise the grade to an 88.5. Out of the 8 homework assignments I had handed in all 8. At the time of the test only a few had been completely correct. However I had been handing in the corrections each day."* So far, so good. The learner added, *"It just took a while to get the homework completely corrected. When I took the test I think had about 3 or 4 completely correct, which could be way I got such a low score on the test, I would miss very minor things on the homework corrections.*

* see resource at www.foreignlanguagesforeveryone.com

I made same mistakes on the test that I made on the homework." Bingo! This student analyzed the personal data and rightly concluded correcting homework does improve test scores because it is far less likely the same mistakes made in the homework will then be made on the exam.

Improving their overall course grade is a strong incentive for students to correct their homework. But there are many ways to try to maximize both students' understanding of the correction-grade connection and their willingness to do corrections as a regular part of their learning. I developed my unique correction method because I believe that fixing the errors on paper (via the tactile mode) also corrects the errors in students' brains. My students know that the payoff for correcting their homework isn't only getting a perfect score on each assignment and thus raising their homework grade, but that there is also a carryover effect to their tests and overall language mastery. I build a lot of palpable incentive into student corrections.

As I wrote in chapter 6, I've found that unlike traditional students— who benefit from quick oral reinforcement of a new concept by doing one or two exercises in the textbook—my students don't find these exercises very helpful for embedding a new concept in their brains. This is probably because students with learning disabilities often have poor auditory processing skills; oral-aural reinforcement activities just don't seem to enhance their understanding. Students who struggle to learn a foreign language need to do these exercises on their own, writing out the answers, in order to highlight the newly taught pattern or concept. The tactile-kinesthetic mode reinforces the concept I'm teaching. Carefully putting their answer in writing makes it far more likely that students will pause and reflect on the new concept.

Perhaps it's better for students to handwrite rather than type homework. Writing embeds tactilely. I encourage typewritten work for students with undecipherable script. I discourage "copying and pasting" repeated phrases when typing or using ditto marks when handwriting. Writing repeated phrases helps embed correct spelling.

Using the IK Correction Method

The IK Correction Method is my most important contribution to teaching my own at-risk students. Although the process is time-consuming, it works so well that I wrote this book partly to share it with other educators.

I first developed it in the early 1970s, when I was teaching small classes of high school French and German. At that time, I began allowing students to correct their homework so that they could learn from their mistakes and repair the misunderstandings lodged in their brains. I came back to the method in 2001, when I began teaching struggling students in my modified foreign-language program—and I also began allowing students to correct tests. I had no idea how helpful it would be for my new educational calling to serve students who were failing or dropping out of foreign-language courses supposedly because they were simply unable to learn a second language.

Each night, in addition to learning a certain number of vocabulary words, reading several sections of the textbook, and sometimes doing listening activities, students write out one or more exercises from the textbook and a few in the workbook. They then self-correct some of the exercises with answer keys. I collect the other, hand-in exercises at the start of the next day's class. Students must put the exercise, page number, and their name at the top of the paper.

Next, I carefully go through each assignment with a red pen, circling all errors of spelling, punctuation, or grammar. I then give a grade out of ten points. I put a red check mark at the top of the paper and record the grade. The next day I give these graded papers* back before class. Students have the opportunity to take the assignment home, make corrections on it, and resubmit it. I instruct them to correct their errors *in situ*, that is, in the exact place where the error was made. They should avoid rewriting an entire sentence (unless instructed to do so), because the possibility of making new errors is too high. After the daily vocabulary quiz, students hand in corrected homework along with the new assignment due that day.

The second time a student hands in an assignment, I go through it with a green pen—a highly visible color. I avoid pastels, which are harder to see. (Be alert to color-blind students—as ascertained from the first-day questionnaire.) I circle remaining errors in green and put a green check at the top of the page to the right of the red check. The following day I once again hand back the corrected paper. And that's not the end of the matter. A student may keep correcting and resubmitting it until they have fixed all of the errors. Moreover, I use a different color of pen for each iteration. I jest with students, "We could be enjoying this together forever, but I don't have

* see resource at www.foreignlanguagesforeveryone.com

enough colors!" I also joke that as long as I still have a few colors left they can continue correcting with hope. Students learn to look at the color of the last check mark to see what still needs to be fixed. Finally, my approach includes this incentive: I don't adjust their grade until they have perfectly completed the entire homework assignment. And what happens to their grade? They receive a perfect score for a perfectly corrected assignment— ten out of ten. Adjusting the grade upward slightly for each improvement of corrections on a homework assignment might induce students to keep trying, but would be a logistical nightmare to track.

So what's going on with my students when I employ the IK Correction Method? For one thing, when students make their own corrections, they start analyzing what they did wrong. They see their work, their correction, and my colored markings side by side. As they review what they see on the paper, they begin repairing not just the assignment but also how their brain processes their own corrections. They dislodge mistakes and begin embedding correct thinking in their brain. For instance, students reexamine their mistaken assumptions about second-language spelling and grammatical patterns. The onus is on them to become independent learners—to figure out what's wrong and to learn how to think and act rightly. Every student who is willing to work hard making corrections is rewarded with a perfect grade on the homework portion of their course grade (15 percent of the overall course grade), regardless of their initial grade on an assignment. So all types of learners have the same chance to earn the same, perfect grade. Each student can then take considerable pride in this achievement for as many assignments as I give for the course. The incentive is considerable. I weigh homework as a hefty percentage of the course grade precisely because I truly believe that corrections help my students learn—even the most challenged second-language learners.

Correcting homework is something that *all* students can do—if only they dedicate the time and put their minds to it. Sometimes students have so many errors on an assignment that correcting them all seems totally overwhelming—at least at first. One of my students journaled, *"I am trying to do better on quizzes and get caught up on homework redoes although I feel like I don't know where to start for the corrections I look at them it seems that so much is wrong and it freaks me out The homework takes me forever."* I encourage students who are feeling overwhelmed to see me—so I can help them identify their needs and encourage them personally. Sometimes I do include a short note on their assignment to explain what they're doing wrong so that they know how to begin making corrections. But I continue encouraging them to see me for any help whatsoever. I want them to know that I desire their success. Also, I often encourage them to work with a tutor.

Of course timeliness is important in learning—assignments and corrections need to go hand in hand for maximum educational gain. I encourage students to make them every day and to get everything fully corrected as soon as possible. A wise student journaled, *"As for homework corrections, I always strive to turn them in the day after I've received the homework back. This way the homework doesn't pile up, and I deal with correcting the mistake in my head right away."* This student exemplifies the pedagogical purpose behind doing homework corrections promptly, while the concepts are still fresh in students' minds so they can immediately benefit from the new knowledge they have acquired.

Unfortunately many at-risk students, especially those with attention issues, have a tendency to procrastinate on the corrections—along with nearly everything else in my courses. Because of this, I put a time limit on homework corrections. I enforce time limits for their own good—not just to keep me from going crazy if I were to receive hundreds of corrected assignments on the last day of the term! The day of a chapter test (e.g., chapter 2) is the last day students may submit any corrections from the previous chapter (e.g., chapter 1). The chapter 3 test day is absolutely the last time I accept anything from chapter 2, and so on. I make sure that the students know the rule about absolute deadlines on the corrections. If students have waited until the last minute to hand in corrections, and the assignments still have errors, then the initial grade holds. I don't give intermediate grades. It's an all-or-nothing approach, but the "all" is truly full credit.

My students quickly see the value of homework corrections. One journaled, *"I believe that in general, people who hand in their homework on-time and correct their homework do better on tests. They get the extra practice from doing their homework and by doing their corrections they can fix any mistakes they are commonly making."* Another student wrote,

I am not doing very well on homework assignments. I have been trying extra hard to get 10 out of 10's but all I get is 7 out of 10. I finally got caught up on correcting old assignments tonight. . . . From now on my goal is to do homework corrections everyday as part of my daily assignments. This will not only keep me caught up, but it will make the corrections easier as the problems will be fresher in my mind.

This student articulated an important fact—doing corrections in a timely fashion fixes errors when they are fresh, thus making them easier to do.

Using the IK Grace Slip Method

Earlier I discussed the tendency of some students to procrastinate and then become overwhelmed as they fall more and more behind on their work. I explained how open-ended grace didn't work because it lacked the boundaries some students need to succeed academically. That's why I developed the IK Grace Slip Method, which I introduced previously. This, too, works well for teaching struggling students. I recommend it enthusiastically.

The IK Grace Slip Method* is somewhat like giving allowances—or indulgences, if you want to think religiously! At the start of each semester, I provide students with twelve grace slips.* They can attach one of those slips to a late assignment for each day that assignment is late; these might include late homework assignments, journal submissions, test corrections, and projects or papers. If a student's assignment is three days late, it will take three grace slips for me to accept that late assignment for full credit. I do accept late submissions without grace slips, but these can receive only half credit (i.e., a maximum of five points out of ten).

A remarkable number of my students never need to use a single grace slip because they keep up with their daily work. One clever student asked in a journal entry whether there could be some kind of reward for students who don't use their grace slips. What a great question! And what a wonderful example of the value of journals for teaching instructors! After some reflection, I decided to give a half point of extra credit on the final exam for each grace slip a student still had at the end of the semester. In other words, a student who didn't use any grace slips during the semester could gain a total of six possible points (out of approximately 200 points) on the final exam. This is a meaningful incentive and can be a considerable boost for students who traditionally don't do well on pencil-and-paper tests. Dare I say that I indulge in a bit in grace?

I love the notion of "grace"—of deep favor toward others. Even governments, banks, and insurance companies offer grace, such as allowing people to pay late for a service, loan, or policy. They legally call it a "grace period." In languages like Spanish and Italian, the word for "thanks" comes from the word that also means "grace"—*gracias* and *grazie* from the Latin *grātia*. I purposely chose this word for the slips because it's so richly meaningful. The idea of grace is one of the most significant philosophical underpinnings of the worldview that underlies my entire pedagogical approach. To me, grace is something undeserved—it is an unmerited gift, extended by the giver out of love rather than out of any required or even expected personal gain. To use Parker J. Palmer's language, teaching with grace affirms the "heart and soul" of education.[6] A charitable approach to teaching and learning resonates perfectly with my overall methodology, which arose out of my desire to help struggling students. The system of grace slips extends grace regardless of the reason for handing something in late—and I don't have to determine if the student has a valid reason for the late submission. Yet it still sets the limits that students need, since there are only twelve slips for an entire semester and I give homework daily.

If students are sick and thus absent from class, they do not need to attach a grace slip to assignments they missed when they were gone. They can simply hand them in without a grace slip when they return. I trust them to not abuse that additional kind of grace. I keep close tabs on absences every day, marking them in my book and on my homework grade sheet. That way I immediately know if an assignment was turned in late due to an absence or was just late. I can then calculate back how many grace slips a student might need for an assignment that was due, for example, five days earlier, three days of which the student was absent. Then only two slips are needed.

If a student has a long bout with illness and misses a lot of work, I ask that student to meet with me to put together a recovery plan with specific due dates for missed assignments. This gives students a framework in which to be successful. Otherwise they often become overwhelmed while trying to catch up.

* see resource at www.foreignlanguagesforeveryone.com

Strategizing for Tests

I address a number of testing issues throughout the year. As I discuss a little later in this chapter, I provide pretests for my students—something they find extremely helpful. In addition to providing study guidelines, I offer students test-taking strategies, especially as we are going through the pretest together. Moreover, I permit students to correct their tests. Before the first one, I give students specific guidelines* on *how* and *what* to study. I stress the importance of thoroughly knowing vocabulary, since words are the building blocks of language. I also give them practical suggestions* for studying vocabulary. I want them to know that I want them to succeed—and that I am going to teach them how to do so, as well as teach them another language and culture.

During the course of the year, the students and I discuss good test-taking tactics. I explain the importance of writing down the four key verbs or other important concepts as soon as I give them their test at the beginning of the test day—and not to wait until they get to that part of the exam. I explain that if they immediately write down the concepts they've been studying, they can then refer to this when the related questions come up on the exam. I always give my students a few minutes to write down these important things after handing out the test. I use a number of additional strategies, including KISS, UTTTTTT, RTD, and LAPV. While these may seem obvious to good test takers, many of my students need to be coached in such commonsense approaches. I know that some of my students learn these for the first time and then begin using them in other classes as well.

- *KISS* (Keep It Simple, Silly). My students often feel compelled to write more than they need to in order to answer a question, as if the more they write the higher their grade will be. For example, if the question is, "*Qu'est-ce que vous avez fait hier soir?*" ("What did you do last night?"), the simple and elegant answer would be something like "*J'ai étudié*" ("I studied"). Some students, however, want to write about all of the things they did last night, or they want to express something they don't know how to say yet in the target language.[7]
- *UTTTTTT* (Use The Test To Take The Test). I carefully scrutinize all tests to make sure that they do not, in one section, provide answers for another exercise (e.g., using a verb form somewhere that is required elsewhere on the test in an exercise on verb formation). An astute

student, however, might find the spelling of a word or phrase elsewhere on the test and use it to answer the question on a different part of the same test. I explain to them that this is an especially good strategy on a test asking for open-ended words or phrases (e.g., if students need to write four items that can be bought in a French bakery, one of those items is very likely mentioned elsewhere because book chapters and my lesson plans tend to be thematically cohesive).

- *RTD* (Read The Directions). While this strategy also seems painfully obvious to some, my students frequently need to be reminded to read and to follow through with the specific instructions on the exam. I encourage them to carefully read the directions for each exercise to be sure they know precisely what they need to do. One common error on a reading section is that students will answer the questions in the wrong language. I want students to answer in English so that I can confirm that they have comprehended the passage.

- *LAPV* (Look At Point Values). This strategy helps students determine how much time they should spend on each section of the test. If an exercise is worth only five points out of 100, they shouldn't be spending 20 percent of their time completing that section. Many students have a hard time completing their tests within the allotted time. I emphasize that keeping track of point values should help them to finish in a timely fashion. Some of my students who are eligible for accommodations due to their learning disabilities can arrange with our Student Academic Services office to complete their tests with extended time in a distraction-free environment, after doing the listening sections with the rest of the class.

Correcting Chapter Tests

I apply the IK Correction Method to tests also, giving students a way to correct in their brains the errors they've made. In my first years of teaching, I'd hand back tests and then we would review them together (with me showing students all the right answers) because I wanted students to learn what they had done wrong. But the strong students didn't really need to go over the tests; they quickly understood their errors. The weak students were so discouraged by another bad test score, however, that they sometimes couldn't even follow along with my review. Moreover, they didn't always understand why their answers were wrong even as I explained the correct answers.

As with daily homework corrections, I want students to learn from their test mistakes by taking the time to carefully examine and fix errors so that they learn from them. In order to do so, however, students must figure out what they did wrong in the first place. With some mistakes, students recognize immediately what's wrong. With other errors, they need to puzzle it out, or go back to class notes, the textbook, or perhaps homework assignments.

I grade tests simply by putting a line through errors or circling them. I don't provide the correct answer. I always hand back the test the next day.[8] A student who receives 60 percent (D–) on a one-hundred-point chapter test and corrects all errors can earn back forty points. I then divide that number in half and add the twenty points to the original sixty points for a final grade of 80 percent (B–). Students still have an incentive to study hard because the higher their initial score, the higher their end grade will be. This system motivates students who don't do well on tests to try their best, but it also enables students to improve a low grade. I suspect it also decreases student anxiety to know they can do corrections.

Allowing students to correct their tests enhances their sense of self-efficacy and encourages them to keep working hard. I concur with Nicole Mills, who coordinates the elementary French program at Harvard University, and her colleagues who contend that "students with a strong sense of academic self-efficacy willingly undertake challenging tasks, expend greater effort, show increased persistence in the presence of obstacles, demonstrate lower anxiety levels . . . and self-regulate better than other students."[9] Many of my students have written in their journals that they never do well on pencil-and-paper tests in any class; they study diligently, but often their grades don't reflect their hard work or demonstrate what they've learned. As I mentioned earlier, some students' test anxiety causes their brain to freeze; they can't extract from their memory the things that they knew before the exam. One student recalled studying hard for a test, but then becoming *"all mixed up"* when the test was handed out. *"It was frustrating,"* the student journaled.

I believe that the traditional system of grading students' tests, handing them back, and then reviewing them in class is often an exercise in futility. By contrast, putting the responsibility on the students themselves to correct their errors enables them to become self-directed learners. When they have to figure out and fix their mistakes, students correct their misunderstandings and will be more likely to remember the same material correctly in the future.

In the spirit of healthy boundaries, however, I give students only two class days to correct their tests. They need to make corrections while concepts are still fresh in their minds. One student candidly journaled about my prompt return of graded tests, and then added, *"It is really, really nice to get the test back corrected while you still remember what you were thinking while you wrote the test. I think that it helps me to better make corrections to think in my mind based on what I remember thinking when I got something wrong on the test."*

For each day beyond the two-day limit, students are allowed to use a grace slip to return their corrected tests. When these are returned to me, I go over each test with a green pen, checking to see that the corrections have been made properly. If something is still wrong on the test, I fill in the correct answer. I hand back all tests the following day for students to see their adjusted grade, and then re-collect and file them for safekeeping. If students want to use their tests to study for the final exam, I give them a test packet on the last regular class meeting day of the semester. Packets must be returned to me before students can take their final exam.

Ingenious students have asked whether they might not also be allowed to correct their daily vocabulary quizzes for additional credit. I admire the resourcefulness of the question. Some instructors might be willing to do this, but obviously there is a limit to the amount of work I can do every day. I have to draw the line somewhere.

It's gratifying to see that students who are willing to work hard are indeed rewarded for their efforts. They learn more and gain a better course grade, but they also benefit from an improved sense of self-efficacy.

Supporting Responsible Learning through Feedback, Evaluation, and Grades

Since I seek to make my students responsible for their own learning, I accept the responsibility to equip them to act responsibly. Toward that end, I employ some additional strategies to help students become better learners.

* see resource at www.foreignlanguagesforeveryone.com

Below I discuss three of them: giving immediate feedback, evaluating students in a variety of different formats, and updating students regularly on their grades so they always know where they stand with course work.

Giving Immediate Feedback

Winograd and Hare stress the value of "giving immediate, academically focused feedback and correction, especially when new material is being learned."[10] This is particularly true for at-risk students. Landmark College Spanish professor Eve Leons and her colleagues similarly believe that students benefit from rapid feedback.[11] So despite the amount of work it gives me daily, I grade anything students hand in and return it to them the next class day. This includes vocabulary quizzes, homework assignments, homework corrections, tests, corrected tests, culture points, and biweekly journals. The one exception is students' written projects and papers. In order to grade these consistently, I generally wait until nearly all of these have been presented in class and then grade them all within a week.

Varying Evaluation Formats

I evaluate students in a variety of ways because many at-risk students can't demonstrate their achievement via traditional methods of assessment. Providing a number of different evaluative formats allows students to show me—and themselves—what they do know instead of just what they don't know. I share Jonathan F. Arries's desire to avoid "high-stakes testing."[12] In my opinion, tests and exams are important, but shouldn't constitute a disproportionately large percentage of a course grade. Forty percent of the overall grade in my classes consists of areas in which any student who works hard can earn an A. In a typical semester, these areas would include the following:

- Class attendance/participation (10 percent)
- Effort/attendance at weekly tutoring sessions (5 percent)
- Doing and correcting daily homework (15 percent)
- Completing culture activities (5 percent)
- Writing two weekly journal entries (5 percent)

The other 60 percent of the course grade is constituted as follows:

- Tests (20 to 25 percent)
- Final exam (15 to 20 percent)
- Daily vocabulary quizzes* (10 percent)
- Project* (formal paper/presentation to class) (5 percent)
- Oral exam* (5 percent)

This grading scale means that all students who are willing to work hard every day are able to complete their foreign-language requirement. Those who don't do well on tests can correct them, thereby improving their grade. I assume pedagogically that if students are doing and correcting their daily homework, attending and participating in class and tutoring sessions, and correcting their tests, they will, by the constant repetition and exposure, master a foreign language to an appropriate level of proficiency. Over the many years of teaching this way, I've found this to be true even for students who have dyslexia or severe auditory processing difficulties. Over the years, only three students couldn't complete my sequence: a home-schooled student who learned to read at age twelve; a severely dyslexic, struggling student who made it through the first two semesters in a supreme effort to master the language; and an emotionally impaired student with memory difficulties who was undergoing extensive testing to determine other learning disabilities and genetic issues. Additionally several students discontinued school or the sequence.

Updating Grades Regularly

Students who accept responsibility for their own learning need to know where they stand academically. I give them a grade-update sheet* approximately every two weeks, which they can then compare with their own records to see if they've made all their assignment corrections. My grading software can send grades via e-mail, but each student would have to take the extra step of printing them. Giving them a printout allows me to add comments, questions, and words of encouragement, and to keep a copy for my file as well as send one to Student Academic Services for probationary students. The update shows them anything they still need to complete, such as culture points or journal entries.

Providing Study Aids

Doris M. Downey and Lynn E. Snyder recommend giving students study aids to help them in foreign-language learning.[13] I give my students numerous study aids throughout the semester: a daily gray handout, worksheets, review sheets, and pretests. All of these give students ancillary tools for study and review, extra reinforcement of new concepts, and help in knowing what to study for a test.

Using a Daily Gray Handout

As I explained in chapter 1, I teach for multisensory learning. In addition to using the more traditional auditory mode, I also incorporate visual learning whenever it's appropriate and possible. I teach with overhead transparencies, which include the basic information for the day's lessons. I produce them in PowerPoint and print them to transparencies. You may prefer to project the PowerPoint pages directly from the computer program onto the screen, but then you can't write on the image. The tangible transparencies allow me to write directly on them to add further explanations and examples, as well as to use different colors.

Before using the transparencies in class each day, I give students a copy of them on a daily gray handout* (four overhead transparencies per page—see supplement 1). Students can then follow along and take organized notes as I explain a new concept. The gray handout provides students with an overview of each lesson and serves as a visual organizer, telling students what they need to focus on each day. This organizer is especially helpful for students with attention-deficit hyperactivity disorder (ADHD).[14] The handout includes the daily vocabulary quiz and any songs or other material that might be part of a day's lesson. I also put in the handout any new grammatical or cultural concepts that I will be teaching that day. Students can circle, underline, and add notes to the handout. Students journal about the value of the daily gray handout. One wrote, *"I really like that we get the handouts of all of the overheads so that we can focus more on what is* *being talked about in class and not worrying about whether or not we wrote everything down."*

Preparing Worksheets and Review Sheets

I sometimes prepare worksheets* to accompany a video shown in class, to reinforce a difficult concept, or to give extra practice when the textbook and workbook are inadequate. For example, I use a worksheet when students have just begun to learn how to put together the two major past tenses in French (*Passé Composé* and *Imparfait*). The worksheet includes an activity in which students read through a story in English and decide, given the context, which tense would be more appropriate. I then use a follow-up worksheet with a similar exercise in French.

Just before the comprehensive final exam at the end of the semester, I give students a review sheet that lists all the vocabulary topics, grammatical concepts, and cultural themes for each chapter. Sometimes I make up individual review sheets for large grammatical concepts that span several chapters. For instance, I provide an overview of all the verb tenses studied, including how they're formed, used, and translated into English.

Helping Students with Pretests

Before every test and final exam, I prepare a pretest or sample test so that students can practice each of the kinds of exercises they can expect on all course tests and exams.[15] I believe that students shouldn't be asked to do an exercise on a test if they haven't done the same kind of exercise previously in class or at home. My pretests* look very similar to actual tests, providing excellent practice. Students can see point values for each section, too, so they can determine how to focus their study time. Students receive the pretest two days ahead. They must complete it for homework the day before the test; we review the pretest that day as well. I don't provide listening and reading comprehension practice as part of the pretest, but students do know the context of these exercises from what they see on the pretest. Students can practice their listening skills with recordings that accompany the textbook. We also do a listening comprehension exercise toward the end of each chapter.

* see resource at www.foreignlanguagesforeveryone.com

Each pretest has a question-and-answer section that we complete together in class. I ask students a question in French, and they write an answer in French. If students have a hard time understanding an aural question, I encourage them to write down as much of the question as they can, so that they can puzzle it out more carefully later. Once students have composed an answer, they may then compare their answer with that of a classmate and discuss why they wrote what they did. We then review the answers together. I write every answer on the overhead transparency copy of the pretest. This gives students the visual reinforcement of correct answers.

Setting Reasonably High Standards

I always hold high but attainable standards for my students, telling them that I expect their best effort just as I expect my own. This is one reason why I require students to sign a contract* at the beginning of the course sequence, laying out what I expect of them in terms of class attendance and the like. The contract also serves to remind them of what they should expect of themselves. While the contract states that I expect two hours of homework for each hour of class contact, I'm delighted if they do a bit less, as long as they continue to study daily. Sometimes students mention in their journals that they're spending more than two or three hours per class hour. I encourage those students to come and see me to discuss ways to make their homework load more reasonable. I usually tell students to focus on the required homework exercises that need to be handed in, and to skip the ones that they are to correct themselves with an answer key.

Through their hard work, I want my students to develop the virtues of diligence, patience, courage, empathy, humility, and hope—as outlined in the course syllabus.* The students work hard—and I do too!

The Value of Teaching and Learning with Grace

I've been developing the practices explained in chapters 6 and 7 for about four decades. Some are tried and true methods employed by many master teachers in foreign language and other disciplines. Others are practices that I've developed specifically for teaching students who struggle with foreign-language learning. Some of the things I've tried over the years never did pan out. The best ones came about through continual refinement. I've learned that excellent instruction requires a continual, even lifelong examination of pedagogical practices. My students deserve considerable credit for helping me develop as a teacher. They have taught me—through their journals, conversations, and encouragement over the years—what it means to teach and learn with grace. I offer them my deepest respect and heartfelt gratitude.

8

Celebrating the Gifts of Teaching and Learning

I've witnessed firsthand the growing concern at all educational levels for students with learning disabilities. I've also seen the growing momentum behind educational movements and strategies for including these students in all arenas. For various reasons but for far too long, students with learning disabilities have been largely excluded from foreign-language learning. I believe it's time to take a hard look at our basic pedagogical assumptions and our teaching practices so that we can successfully adapt them to meet the needs of these students. Only then will such students truly enjoy the many benefits of using foreign languages. In our globally oriented world, where we come from all nations, tribes, and peoples, everyone should learn how to interact cross-culturally and linguistically.

Let's do a little exercise together. Please invest a few minutes of your time, focusing on one struggling foreign-language student you've had in your own classroom. Just jot down answers to the following eight questions (a Microsoft Word version is on my website*):

1. What language were you teaching?
2. What was the course level?
3. What kind of pedagogical approach were you using (e.g., TPRS, communicative activities, more traditional grammar-focused, or a mix of these)?

4. Briefly describe the student:
    Age:
    Gender:
    Family background:
    Socioeconomic background:
    Handedness:
    Prior attempts at second-language learning:
    Any other relevant student features or characteristics:
5. What was the nature of the student's learning difficulty (e.g., listening, speaking, reading, writing, grammar, vocabulary, pacing, anxiety, spelling, memorization, or attention)?
6. Was this student receiving any learning-disabilities services?
7. What strategies or accommodations did you employ to help this student?
8. What were the outcomes for this student?

Please set this brief synopsis aside for a moment—we'll come back to it shortly.

I've been richly blessed as a teacher for nearly four decades. I've had the privilege of teaching students from elementary school through graduate school. I've been able to teach not only different languages like French, German, and Dutch, but also how to teach languages. I've learned a great deal from my students at all levels. For instance, while teaching young children in after-school and summer foreign-language programs, I observed the sheer joy of learning a language simply for pleasure—singing songs, reading stories, and learning the colors, numbers, and days of the week—all without the pressure of assigning or receiving grades. I learned from high school and college students that second-language learning is a breeze for some learners and a tremendous struggle for others. The same learning that brings delight and self-confidence to some students can take a real toll on struggling learners' sense of self. I know personally that second-language instruction for at-risk students can be a curse as well as a blessing.

As I explained in the introduction, both personal circumstances and my professional activities led me to have considerable compassion for at-risk foreign-language learners. So I set out to unravel the secrets of successful second-language learning for students who themselves know it doesn't come easily. In my early years, first as a Canadian immigrant and later as an American citizen fluent in various languages, I focused primarily on the strong students—the ones who enjoyed language and did well at it. I must admit that in those early years I was somewhat blind to some of the needs right before me, in my own classrooms. I was barely aware of the weak students, perhaps because I wasn't really sure how to help them. Why worry about something that we can't change? Yet there was always a small, persistently growing warm spot in my heart for the struggling students. They were such fine people. They were so obviously good at so many other things. I increasingly wondered why foreign-language learning was so hard and painful for them, especially when it was so easy and fun for me.

I learned, too, that many other educators shared my compassion for such wonderful but challenged students. The more I spoke up about the needs of at-risk second-language learners, the more individuals I discovered who had similar desires to serve this group. In fact, I received wonderful feedback on this book from my own graduate students. They were the first to read my nascent ideas in manuscript form, and they helped me refine and improve my initial writing of this book so that others could benefit from my experiences. This shared sense of joy in and compassion for at-risk second-language learners can be contagious. Knowing and serving these students can give us educators tremendous, heartfelt rewards.

So I offer deep gratitude to those struggling students who have allowed me to learn by granting me the privilege of learning with them. Even though I taught them from a strong theoretical research base, the students courageously joined me on the daily journey of discovery. They truly showed me the way. They worked so hard and gave so much of themselves to my unfolding project. They were unfailingly honest about how my instruction was affecting them—what worked and what didn't, and what I could do differently, better, more compassionately, more justly, more patiently, more genuinely. They wrote candid, insightful journals about their sense of self-efficacy—what they thought they could do and what they couldn't. One student journaled:

> *This is the last French journal I am ever likely to write. . . . It seems like a long time ago that I wrote the first one, but it has gone by pretty quickly. Prior to entering the classes this year I was seriously wondering how I was*

going to manage to get the foreign language requirement out of the way without killing my GPA. I guess I found out how. I must apologize at this point, I thought that these French classes were going to be awful. I was really not very pleased with the sound of them after our brief interview last year. To my mind they sounded wishy-washy, boring and above all useless. I was profoundly mistaken. The structure of these classes was anything but wishy-washy, nor was the content anything of the sort. The grading was difficult, yet incredibly gracious in it us of opportunities for correction. I did not find them boring either, instead I found learning French to be rather enjoyable and quite interesting in a number of ways, much to my surprise. I have also changed my tune on the usefulness of these courses. I am not very likely to use the French I learned on any real regular basis, however, I think that I am probably better off for having learned it. If for no other reason than that having to learn a new language has caused me to look at the ways in which I use my native language and thus expand my capabilities for expressing ideas. In addition, I think that French actually helped me out in some of my other classes. . . . I am still somewhat astounded by how effectively these classes taught French. I recall that trying to learn German freshman year was akin to pulling teeth. I don't think that the two classes were all that dissimilar, outside of the size, but there is quite obviously something (or some number of things) very different about the way that they function. The little elements of organizational difference and size and teaching style evidently influence the way a course functions to teach students vastly more than I would have guessed possible. I think that the work of prof. Konyndyk made a huge difference too. I suspect that she probably worked harder to teach us French than any of us worked to learn it.

What can or should I say about such a journal entry? About such a student? Who am I to have been blessed by a learner who transformed a mere academic requirement into a blessed life experience? I couldn't help but wonder what would happen to this at-risk learner. What would the future look like? Now I know. This at-risk student eventually went to medical school, grew greatly in knowledge of French and of self, and is living as a gifted learner. I could learn much from such a former student. Actually I learn much from these students daily in my classroom. I've also learned that my own students will become the kinds of mature people who care for others. This student became the kind of physician that we want to be our own doctor.

Witnessing the life stories of former students is part of the joy of teaching a second language to those who supposedly can't learn one, who supposedly lack the capacity, ability, or motivation. Their learning difficulties are real. But so is their desire to learn. They are students who in the process of learning what they supposedly can't learn benefit the most from overcoming obstacles. From persisting. From eventually succeeding. We all benefit from their learning—and from their participation in society. Their "different" minds—their attention-deficit issues, their autism, and all of the other "isms"—are part of the human capacity to serve and to be served. They include the likes of Albert Einstein, Louis Pasteur, John F. Kennedy, Winston Churchill, General George Patton, John Lennon, F. Scott Fitzgerald, Whoopi Goldberg, Leonardo da Vinci, Charles Schwab, Mozart, and Galileo.

In addition to what I've learned from my students, I've also gained much from scholars who carry on research and share their results with the rest of us. They continue to pursue important questions, and their answers, tentative as they might be at times, enrich teaching and learning for us all. There are so many avenues for future research. The latest developments in neuroscience and magnetic resonance imagery, for example, are showing us how different areas of the brain are activated with different kinds of learning. What might the impact of that research be? How does music affect foreign-language learning? How might the olfactory sense be incorporated? Is there a relation between mathematical learning, for example, and foreign-language learning? What is it about foreign-language learning that makes it so difficult for the same people who eventually go on to become entrepreneurs, inventors, artists, and computer geeks? I'd love to see more interdisciplinary collaboration (e.g., between foreign languages and psychology), increased cooperation between the foreign-language and learning-disabilities communities, and more interaction between scholars and classroom teachers. In this book, I've attempted to bridge some of these divides.

I've also sought in this book to show how scholarly research supports changes in teaching practice—to bring theory and praxis together in real and tangible ways. Students with learning disabilities often do struggle to become proficient in foreign languages, but it truly is possible for them to do so, if we're willing to adapt our teaching approaches to meet their needs. But first, we need to be more aware of the different kinds of learners we have in our classrooms—they are indeed already there, waiting and desiring to learn! We need to determine what they need in order to be successful. And then we need to provide avenues for them to do so. Some people say that providing accommodations for students with learning disabilities is simply "leveling the playing field." I agree. But I also think that what we learn from them about teaching will help us to better serve all students. Frequently those in society who seem to be the weakest among us are the very ones who have so much more to offer. They humble us.

Weaving the Golden Thread of Learning

Now look again at the brief student synopsis you wrote at the start of this chapter. Of the many strategies presented in this book, which ones might have helped your student? Which ideas can you incorporate into your general teaching practice right now? Start small. Experiment. Be patient with yourself and your learners. Form a learning community. Encourage candid journaling. Let your students tell you what they would find helpful. Then start savoring even the small successes. Continue enlarging your thinking. Interact with other teachers in your field and beyond. Converse with learning-disabilities professionals and resource room teachers. Above all, let your classroom be a place where a lovely golden thread is beautifully woven into the tapestry of your students' lives, and where even the most at-risk student can say: "*I have learned that I am capable of learning a foreign language.*"

Supplement 1
Daily Gray Sheet Sample

Dans le sac à dos

- un cahier   a notebook
- une calculatrice =
- des ciseaux   some scissors
- un crayon   a pencil
- un livre   a book
- un sac à dos   a backpack
- un stylo   a pen

French 111-Konyndyk

avoir = to have
[TB p. 53]

- j'ai   nous avons

- tu as   vous avez

- il, elle, on a   ils, elles ont

e.g.
- J'ai un crayon.
- Est-ce que vous avez un ordinateur?
- Elle n'a **pas de** livre.

French 111-Konyndyk

- **NOTES**:
1. In the negative, *pas* + *un, une* or *des* ==> **pas de** ["not any; no"]!!
- This often occurs with the verb *avoir*.
e.g.   Tu as une moto?
       Non, je n'ai **pas de** moto.
2. There are many common **expressions** with *avoir*:
- *avoir besoin de*   (to need) [lit.: to have need of]
- *avoir faim*   (to be hungry) [lit.: to have hunger]
- *avoir soif*   (to be thirsty) [lit.: to have thirst]

French 111-Konyndyk

♫ *"pas de"* Chant ♪

- ♫ ♪ *Pas de, pas de, pas de,* ♪

- ♫ *un, une, des* become *de* after *pas!* ♪♫

French 111-Konyndyk

Supplement 2
First-Day Questionnaire

QUESTIONNAIRE FOR FRENCH 111 [All information will be kept **confidential**]

Name (Full name *and* the name by which you want to be called):

Tell me something that will help me remember **who** you are:

Local Address & Phone #:

E-mail Address (**Add **"NOTE" if different from campus e-mail**):

Class Level:

Major: Minor (if applicable):

Place and date of birth:

High school attended (Name and city):

Family info (Parents, sibs, etc.):

Career goals:

What do you like to do in your free time?

Do you read in your spare time? If so, what kinds of things?

What do you hope to **gain from** taking French 111?

What do you hope to **give** to this class?

What are your goals for this course?

Discuss the following: How do you expect French to be taught from a **Christian perspective**? Do you think this French class might be different from a similar class taught at a secular university? If so, how?

What is your favorite subject and why?

What is your **least** favorite subject and why?

Give 3 words to describe yourself:

How do you learn best? How would you describe your learning style? Visual? Auditory? Kinesthetic? Other?

What would a person who knows you well say that you excel in?

Have you had any musical training? If so, please describe.

Do you recall any incident from your prior schooling where you were put down academically? How did that make you feel?

Do you recall any incident from your prior schooling where you were really successful academically? How did that make you feel?

Describe your experience in high school with grammar instruction.

How did you do in your reading, writing, and literature classes?

How did you do in social studies?

Have some areas remained difficult and others not?

Outline any previous foreign language learning experience you have had (elementary school, high school, college) —list language and explain setting.

Were there any specific things that made foreign language learning difficult for you? Explain.

How would you rate your English **spelling** ability, on a scale of 1 (poor) to 10 (excellent)?

How would you rate your English **grammar** ability, on a scale of 1 (poor) to 10 (excellent)?

How would you rate your English **reading** ability, on a scale of 1 (poor) to 10 (excellent)?

How would you rate your **memorization** ability, on a scale of 1 (poor) to 10 (excellent)?

How many hours per day do you study?

* Do your study habits vary from subject to subject? If so, describe.

- What is difficult for you to study and why?

- Do you consider yourself a good writer?   Explain:

- How you would rate your (English) pronunciation? Can people usually understand you when you speak?

- How would you rate your ability to memorize and recall numbers, dates, names, days of the week, and months?

- Are you often late for appointments, deadlines, etc.? Explain.

- Do you ever write things on your hand to remember them?

- How would you rate your sense of direction?   How would you rate your sense of left / right or north/south and east/west?   Can you read a map upside down?

- When you have a task that requires a lot of thought, do you avoid or delay getting started? Explain.

- Do you often fidget or squirm with your hands or feet when you have to sit down for a long time? Explain.

- Do you ever feel overly active and compelled to do things, like you were driven by a motor?

- Are you color-blind?

- How would you rate your sense of smell?

- Do you have any food allergies? Explain.

- Do you have any allergies (other than food)? Explain.

- Do you often misplace things like keys, papers, etc.? Explain.

- Do you ever go to get something and then forget what you went to get? Explain.

- Do you get mixed up when you are given 3 or more things to do in a row? Explain.

- Do you have trouble wrapping up the final details of a project, once the challenging parts have been done?
- Do you have difficulty getting things in order when you have to do a task that requires organization?
- Do you have any difficulty telling time unless the clock is digital? Explain.

- Do you use memory strategies? Explain.

- Do you have a relative who has (had) reading / writing problems? Other learning difficulties? Explain.

- Have any of your family members been identified as having a learning difficulty? AD(H)D?   If so, who?

- Are you currently taking medication for your learning difficulties?   If so, what?

    When do you take it?   Do you find it helpful?
    Are there any negative side effects?

- Sleep patterns:

    - How many hours do you usually sleep per night?

    - Regular restful sleep?   If no, please explain:

    - Hard time falling asleep?   If yes, please explain:

    - Hard time getting up in the morning?   If yes, please explain:

    - Sleep apnea?

    - Other comments:

- Are you: left-handed?   right-handed?   ambidextrous?

Childhood "stuff":

  - At what age did you learn to walk?   to talk?

  - Did you ever have speech therapy?   Eye-tracking therapy?

  - Did you have ear infections as a child? (If so, how severely? Tubes?)

  - How old you were when you learned to read?

  - Did you enjoy reading? Why, or why not?

  - Do you remember the method by which you learned to read in school? (Phonics? Whole language?)

  - Were you a good speller?   Are you a good speller now?

  - Have you ever had a concussion or head injury?   If so, how many times?

Do the following characteristics generally describe you (not only in an academic setting)?

impulsive	difficulty with concentration/focus
spacey/daydreaming	hyperactive
distractible	depressed
procrastinator	difficulty with organization/time
effective study habits	addictive behaviors (Explain)

Are there any health issues that might impede your success in this class?

How would you describe your learning difficulties in general?

Do you have any concerns about this course? Explain.

Online Appendixes

These appendixes are available for download at
www.foreignlanguagesforeveryone.com.

Appendix A: Description of Modified Foreign Language Program and Process for Student Admission
An outline of the program and the steps students need to take for admission.

Appendix B: Content of Student Interview
A list of the questions I ask students during their admission interview.

Appendix C: Copy of Student Contract
A teacher-student contract that tells students what they need to do (e.g., active participation, class attendance, completion of homework, tutoring) in order to be successful in the program.

Appendix D: Sample of a Day's Homework Assignment
A typical day's homework assignment, which includes a new journal question, vocabulary to learn, textbook exercises to complete, and workbook exercises to complete and self-correct.

Appendix E: Guidelines for Journal Submissions
A handout that explains the basic purpose of keeping a journal and provides guidelines, due dates, suggested topics, and the grading rubric.

Appendix F: Vowel and Consonant Sheets
A list of all the regular and nasal vowel sounds in French, as well as the consonants, phonetic transcriptions, the various spellings of each sound, and examples of each.

Appendix G: Suggestions for Studying the Vocabulary Words
A handout with suggestions for how to study vocabulary, such as covering up words and testing knowledge, writing words out multiple times, and using highlighter pens to color-code word genders.

Appendix H: Characteristics of Good Language Learners
A handout listing some of the characteristics of good second-language learners, such as being willing to make mistakes, looking for patterns, paying attention to meaning, and looking for opportunities to use the language.

Appendix I: Study Hints for Learning a Second Language
A handout of hints for successful second-language study, such as listening and imitating, memorizing, studying out loud, breaking materials down into small units, using class time well, avoiding cramming, thinking and analyzing, and making intelligent guesses.

Appendix J: Sample of Instructions for a Tutoring Session
An explanation of activities for one of the first tutoring sessions of the academic year, focusing primarily on pronunciation.

Appendix K: Sample of Course Syllabus
Basic course information, such as how to contact me, required course materials, course expectations, a statement on academic integrity, an assessment rubric, additional course policies, and a specific outline of semester dates for tests, exams, and journal due dates.

Appendix L: Sample of Student's Homework Assignment with an Initial Grade out of Ten and a Grace Slip
A typical student homework assignment with a starting grade of eight out of ten on it, as well as a grace slip because it was submitted a day late.

Appendix M: Sample of Grace Slips and Instructions for Using Them
An explanation of how grace slips can be used, along with the twelve grace slips available for one semester.

Appendix N: Sample of "How to Study for a Test"
A handout with very specific student instructions on how and what to study for a test, including vocabulary, grammar, listening, and culture.

Appendix O: Sample of Homework Update Sheet
A sample student grade update listing homework grades, as well as quizzes, tests, and other assignments.

Notes

To assist readers in finding full documentation, a cross-reference to the full citation is provided in parentheses at the end of each short reference.

Introduction: Reaching Out to Our Struggling Second-Language Learners

1. "In 2007–08, some 39 percent of all children and youth [ages three to twenty-one] receiving services under IDEA (Individuals with Disabilities Education Act) had specific learning disabilities, and 22 percent had speech or language impairments." See Susan Aud et al., "Participation in Education," in *The Condition of Education 2010*, sec. 1 (Washington, DC: National Center for Education Statistics, Institute of Education Sciences, US Department of Education, 2010), 34, http://nces.ed.gov/pubs2010/2010028_2.pdf. Of incoming freshman in 2008, 3.3 percent reported having a learning disability—up steadily from 0.5 percent in 1983. See "The American Freshman: National Norms Fall 2010," *HERI Research in Brief*, January 2011, 2, http://www.heri.ucla.edu/PDFs/pubs/briefs/brief-pr012208-08FreshmanNorms.pdf.

2. Sharon M. DiFino and Linda J. Lombardino, "Language Learning Disabilities: The Ultimate Foreign Language Challenge," *Foreign Language Annals* 37 (2004): 397.

3. Margaret A. Crombie, "The Effects of Specific Learning Difficulties (Dyslexia) on the Learning of Foreign Language in School," *Dyslexia* 3 (1997): 44; Jean Robertson, "The Neuropsychology of Modern Foreign Language Learning," in *Multilingualism, Literacy and Dyslexia: A Challenge for Educators*, ed. Lindsay Peer and Gavin Reid (London: David Fulton, 2000), 209.

4. The US Department of Education offers a fairly long definition of a learning-disabled student. See US Department of Education, "Identification of Specific Learning Disabilities," Department of Education website, published online October 4, 2006, http://idea.ed.gov/explore/view/p/%2Croot%2Cdynamic%2CTopicalBrief%2C23%2C. The National Center for Learning Disabilities cites the general federal definition of specific learning disabilities: "The term means a disorder in one or more of the basic psychological processes involved in understanding or in using language, spoken or written, that may manifest itself in an imperfect ability to listen, think, speak, read, write, spell, or to do mathematical calculations, including conditions such as perceptual disabilities, brain injury, minimal brain dysfunction, dyslexia, and developmental aphasia." The federal definition says a learning disability doesn't include "learning problems that are primarily the result of visual, hearing, or motor disabilities, of mental retardation, of emotional disturbance, or of environmental, cultural, or economic disadvantage." See Candace Cortiella, "Study Supports Improved Ways to Identify Learning Disabilities," National Center for Learning Disabilities website, published online March 4, 2009, http://www.ncld.org/ld-basics/ld-explained/basic-facts/study-supports-improved-ways-to-identify-learning-disabilities.

5. NJCLD is a "national committee of representatives of organizations committed to the education and welfare of individuals with learning disabilities." See "National Joint Committee on Learning Disabilities," LD Online, http://www.ldonline.org/about/partners/njcld.

6. Richard L. Sparks, "Intelligence, Learning Disabilities, Attention Deficit Hyperactivity Disorder, and Foreign Language Learning Problems: A Research Update," *ADFL Bulletin* 36, no. 2 (2005): 47; Dorcas Francisco, "Learning Disabilities and the Foreign Language Classroom," *Language Resource Newsletter*, 2005, 6; Richard L. Sparks, Elke Schneider, and Leonore Ganschow, "Teaching Foreign (Second) Language to At-Risk Learners," in *Literacy and the Second Language Learner*, ed. JoAnn Hammadou Sullivan (Greenwich, CT: Information Age, 2002), 55–83; Richard L. Sparks et al., "Native Language Predictors of Foreign Language Proficiency and Foreign Language Aptitude," *Annals of Dyslexia* 56 (2006): 129–60.

7. Jonathan F. Arries, "Learning Disabilities and Foreign Languages: A Curriculum Approach to the Design of Inclusive Courses," *Modern Language Journal* 83 (1999): 98–110; Kenneth T. Dinklage, "The Inability to Learn a Foreign Language," in *Emotional Problems of*

the Student, ed. Graham Blaine and Charles MacArthur (New York: Appleton-Century-Crofts, 1971), 185–206; Anna H. Gajar, "Foreign Language Learning Disabilities: The Identification of Predictive and Diagnostic Variables," *Journal of Learning Disabilities* 20, no. 6 (1987): 327–30; Leonore Ganschow and Richard L. Sparks, "'Foreign' Language Learning Disabilities: Issues, Research, and Teaching Implications," in *Success for College Students with Learning Disabilities*, ed. S. Vogel and Pamela Adelman (New York: Springer, 1993), 283–320; Irene Brouwer Konyndyk, "Teaching French (and Spanish) to Students with Dyslexia: Comparative Perspectives" (paper presented at the International Dyslexia Association Conference, Washington, DC, June 2002); Irene Brouwer Konyndyk, "Direct and Explicit Instruction in the Foreign Language Classroom: Showing Hospitality to Students with Learning Disabilities," *Journal of Christianity and Foreign Languages* 12 (2011): 79–85; Paul Pimsleur, Donald Sundland, and Ruth McIntyre, "Underachievement in Foreign Language Learning," *International Review of Applied Linguistics* 2 (1964): 113–50; Elke Schneider, "Foreign Language Learning and Learning Disabilities: Instructional Alternatives" (workshop presented at the Foreign Language Forum of Calvin College, Grand Rapids, MI, October 1998); Sparks, "Intelligence," 43–50 (see intro., n. 6); Richard L. Sparks, Leonore Ganschow, and Jane Pohlman, "Linguistic Coding Deficits in Foreign Language Learners," *Annals of Dyslexia* 39 (1989): 179–95; Susan Vogel et al., "Students with Learning Disabilities in Higher Education: Faculty Attitude and Practices," *Learning Disabilities Research and Practice* 14, no. 3 (1999): 173–86.

8. Richard L. Sparks and Leonore Ganschow, "Foreign Language Learning Differences: Affective or Native Language Aptitude Differences?" *Modern Language Journal* 75 (Spring 1991): 3–16; Sparks, Ganschow, and Pohlman, "Linguistic Coding," 179–95 (see intro., n. 7).

9. Richard L. Sparks, "Foreign Language Learning Problems of Students Classified as Learning Disabled and Non–Learning Disabled: Is There a Difference?" *Topics in Language Disorders* 21, no. 2 (2001): 38–54.

10. Richard L. Sparks, "At-Risk Second Language Learners: Problems, Solutions, and Challenges," *Foreign Language Annals* 42 (2009): 4. See also Elena L. Grigorenko, "Foreign Language Acquisition and Language-Based Learning Disabilities," in *Individual Differences and Instructed Language Learning*, ed. Peter Robinson (Amsterdam: John Benjamins, 2002), 95–112.

Chapter 1: Engaging Students in Multisensory Ways

1. I thank James K. Smith for this idea.

2. Sparks and colleagues explain the difficulties poor foreign-language learners have with putting sounds and symbols together to form words. They also discuss "tasks involving phonological/orthographic processing." They summarize multisensory structured language teaching as "explicit, multisensory, structured." See Sparks, Schneider, and Ganschow, "Teaching Foreign (Second) Language," 62, 69 (see intro., n. 6). See also Richard L. Sparks et al., "Use of an Orton-Gillingham Approach to Teach a Foreign Language to Dyslexic/LD Students: Explicit Teaching of Phonology in a Second Language," *Annals of Dyslexia* 41 (1991): 97–118; Betty B. Sheffield, "The Structured Flexibility of Orton-Gillingham," *Annals of Dyslexia* 41 (1991): 41–54; Curtis W. McIntyre and Joyce S. Pickering, "Multisensory Structured Language Programs: Content and Principles of Instruction," International Multisensory Structured Language Education Council (IMSLEC) (1995), http://www.ldonline.org/article/6332; Madeline Ehrman, "The Modern Language Aptitude Test for Predicting Learning Success and Advising Students," *Applied Language Learning* 9, nos. 1 and 2 (1998): 31–70; Arries, "Learning Disabilities," 98–110 (see intro., n. 7). "Results from their studies showed three principles that were associated with successful learning: multisensory teaching should be used wherever possible, overhead transparencies (OHTs) should support oral language and that grapho-phonic conversion should be taught explicitly." See Robertson, "Neuropsychology," 209 (see intro., n. 3).

3. Also see the Orton-Gillingham method. Elke Schneider, *Multisensory Structured Metacognitive Instruction: An Approach to Teaching a Foreign Language to At-Risk Students* (Hamburg, Germany: Peter Lang, 1999). On learning styles and preferences, see Anna U. Chamot, "The Learning Strategies of ESL Students," in *Learner Strategies in Language Learning*, ed. Anita Wenden and J. Rubin (London: Prentice Hall, 1987), 71–83; Elaine K. Horwitz, "The Beliefs about Language Learning of Beginning University Foreign Language Students," *Modern Language Journal* 72 (1988): 28–94; Judith L. Shrum and Elaine W. Glisan, *Teacher's Handbook:*

Contextualized Language Instruction (Boston: Heinle & Heinle, 1994), 199–224; Doris M. Downey and Lynn E. Snyder, "College Students with Learning Language–Learning Disorders: The Phonological Core as Risk for Failure in Foreign Language Classes," *Topics in Language Disorders* 21, no. 1 (2000): 82–92; Suzanne Graham, "Learners' Metacognitive Beliefs: A Modern Foreign Languages Case Study," *Research in Education* 70, no. 2 (2003): 9–20; Rebecca Oxford, "Styles, Strategies, and Aptitude: Connections for Languages in the United States," in *Language Aptitude Reconsidered*, ed. Thomas Parry and Charles Stansfield (Englewood Cliffs, NJ: Prentice Hall, 2005), 67–125; Howard Gardner, *Intelligence Reframed: Multiple Intelligences for the 21st Century* (New York: Basic Books, 1999); Howard Gardner, *Multiple Intelligences: The Theory in Practice* (New York: Basic Books, 1993). On music, see Katie Overy, "Dyslexia and Music: From Timing Deficits to Musical Intervention," *Annals of the New York Academy of Sciences* 999 (2003): 497–505.

4. Barbro B. Johansson, "Cultural and Linguistic Influence on Brain Organization for Language and Possible Consequences for Dyslexia: A Review," *Annals of Dyslexia* 56, no. 1 (2006): 14, 37. Also consult Yim-Chi Ho, Cheung Mei-Chun, and Agnes S. Chan, "Music Training Improves Verbal but Not Visual Memory: Cross-Sectional and Longitudinal Explorations in Children," *Neuropsychology* 17, no. 3 (2003): 439–50; Andrea R. Kilgour, Lorna S. Jakobson, and Lola L. Cuddy, "Music Training and Rate of Presentation as Mediator of Text and Song Recall," *Memory and Cognition* 28 (2000): 700–710; Danielle Schön, Cyrille Magne, and Mireille Besson, "The Music of Speech: Music Training Facilitates Pitch Processing in Both Music and Language," *Psychophysiology* 41 (2004): 34–49; William Forde Thompson, E. Glenn Schellenberg, and Gabriela Husain, "Perceiving Prosody in Speech: Effects of Music Lessons," *Annals of the New York Academy of Sciences* 999 (2003): 530–32; William Forde Thompson, E. Glenn Schellenberg, and Gabriela Husain, "Decoding Speech Prosody: Do Music Lessons Help?" *Emotion* 4 (2004): 46–64; Stefan Koelsch et al., "Music, Language, and Meaning: Brain Signatures of Semantic Processing," *Nature Neuroscience* 7 (2004): 302–7; Burkhard Maess et al., "Musical Syntax Is Processed in Broca's Area: An MEG Study," *Nature Neuroscience* 4 (2001): 540–45.

5. Oliver Sacks, "When Music Heals," *Parade*, March 31, 2002, 4–5.

6. In French, the letters *e* and *i* can be quite tricky as well as the letters *g* and *j*.

7. Four on a page works well. Six makes the font too small. Three, with lines for notes, uses excess paper.

8. Vocabulary sheets are pink; homework assignments (done for an entire chapter at a time) are purple; the daily sheet is gray; worksheets are blue.

9. Mel Levine, *A Mind at a Time* (New York: Simon and Schuster, 2002), 165.

10. Research supports using highlighters. See Robertson, "Neuropsychology," 202–10 (see intro., n. 3). Using pictures for vocabulary items is extremely helpful at the elementary level; they can be used on smaller flash cards or on larger posters around the room.

11. Wendy Maxwell's Accelerative Integrated Method (AIM) for teaching French to Canadian elementary students employs hand gestures with all words spoken in class. Classes are conducted entirely in French, and students learn the gestures along with the teacher. Students eventually no longer need the gestures. See http://www.aimlanguagelearning.com/.

12. Gardner, *Intelligence Reframed*, 31–105 (see chap. 1, n. 3).

13. In French, each short phrase has a rising pattern and the final phrase has a falling pattern. In English, the equivalent would be "I went to the store, ↑ I bought some bread, ↑ and then I went home." ↓

14. I thank Kara Feikema for this idea.

15. These would be especially helpful for schools with block scheduling, where class periods are longer than a typical fifty-minute time frame.

16. Sparks, Schneider, and Ganschow, "Teaching Foreign (Second) Language," 71 (see intro., n. 6).

17. "Odors . . . call up the entire ambience of an experience—not just what you saw, but how you felt at the time. That is why the smell of a baking apple pie can immediately bring back memories of a childhood Thanksgiving at grandmother's house." See Claudia Dreifus, "The Sweet Smell of Success," *AARP Bulletin*, October 2005, 26–27. Dreifus refers to the work of biologist Linda B. Buck, who, along with Richard Axel of Columbia University, won the Nobel Prize in physiology or medicine in 2004 for showing how olfaction works in mice and humans.

18. Amanda E. Amend et al., "A Modified Spanish Sequence for Students with Language-Based Learning Disabilities," *Foreign Language Annals* 42, no. 1 (2009): 43; Diane A. Ackerman, *A Natural History of the Senses* (New York: Vintage Books, 1990).

19. Edwin T. Morris, "The Importance of Olfaction, Key Sense in Scent," in *Fragrance: The Story of Perfume from Cleopatra to Chanel* (New York: Charles Scribner's Sons, 1984), 35–52.

Chapter 2: Providing Parameters for Student Success

1. Schneider uses the term "Multisensory Structured Language" to suggest that teachers should "organize the learning into small units that present and practice the rules in a logical, explicit fashion." See *Multisensory*, 65 (see chap. 1, n. 3). The use of highly structured and carefully progressing units in sequence and for mastery is discussed in Sparks, Schneider, and Ganschow, "Teaching Foreign (Second) Language, 55–83 (see intro., n. 6).

2. Levine attributes the terms "brain recess" and "mind break" to educator Nan Murphy. See Levine, *Mind at a Time*, 73 (see chap. 1, n. 9).

3. Mel Levine, "How Does Studying Just Before Sleep Help Learning?," WebMD website, published online December 31, 2008, http://answers.webmd.com/answers/1183247/How-does-studying-just-before-sleep.

4. Speaking should be assessed from time to time. Students could record their speaking for you to listen to later. You might conduct a brief speaking test with individual students while the others are writing.

5. In French, "I would work" is written *je travaillerais*; many students think they're saying "I would *travel*" when they write this because the French word looks like "travel." Etymologically the root of the word *travailler* is the same as that of the old English word *travail*. Students should write *je voyagerais* if they want to say "I would *travel*."

6. Levine, *Mind at a Time*, 71 (see chap. 1, n. 9).

7. Peter Winograd and Victoria Chou Hare, "Direct Instruction of Reading Comprehension Strategies: The Nature of Teacher Explanation," in *Learning and Study Strategies: Issues in Assessment, Instruction, and Evaluation*, ed. Claire E. Weinstein and Ernest T. Goetz (San Diego, CA: Academic Press, 1988), 122.

8. Amend and colleagues call this "the repetition needed to develop automaticity." See Amend et al., "Modified Spanish Sequence," 29 (see chap. 1, n. 18).

9. Levine, *Mind at a Time*, 157, 165 (see chap. 1, n. 9).

Chapter 3: Getting to Know Students through a Survey

1. Parker J. Palmer, *To Know as We Are Known: Education as a Spiritual Journey* (San Francisco: Harper & Row, 1983), xvi.

2. Henri J. Nouwen, *Reaching Out: The Three Movements of the Spiritual Life* (Garden City, NY: Image Books, 1986), 86–87.

3. Franz E. Weinert and Rainer H. Kluwe, introduction to *Metacognition, Motivation and Understanding*, ed. Franz E. Weinert and Rainer H. Kluwe (Hillsdale, NJ: Erlbaum, 1987), xi.

4. Scott G. Paris and Peter Winograd, "How Metacognition Can Promote Academic Learning and Instruction," in *Dimension of Thinking and Cognitive Instruction*, ed. Beau Fly Jones and Lorna Idol (Hillsdale, NJ: Erlbaum, 1990), 43.

5. John H. Flavell, "Metacognition and Cognitive Monitoring: A New Area of Cognitive-Developmental Inquiry," *American Psychologist* 34, no. 10 (1979): 906–11.

6. Larry Vandergrift, "It Was Nice to See That Our Predictions Were Right: Developing Metacognition in L2 Listening Comprehension," *Canadian Modern Language Review* 58, no. 4 (2002): 557, 559.

7. Anita Wenden, "Metacognitive Knowledge and Language Learning," *Applied Linguistics* 19 (1998): 518, 530–31.

8. Douglas J. Palmer and Ernest T. Goetz, "Selection and Use of Study Strategies: The Role of the Studier's Beliefs about Self and Strategies," in *Learning and Study Strategies: Issues in Assessment, Instruction, and Evaluation*, ed. Claire E. Weinstein, Ernest T. Goetz, and Patricia A. Alexander (Gainesville, FL: Florida Academic Press, 1988), 41–42.

9. Summarizing the research, Schneider reports, "Generally, metacognition refers to the ability to think about thinking. . . . In the specific context of language learning, metacognitive

skills refer to the ability to reflect about language concepts. These concepts involve phonology/orthography, syntax, morphology, semantics, and pragmatics. The learner who doesn't generalize language patterns independently needs help in directly becoming aware of why and when certain linguistic actions take place. . . . This help is provided by the teacher and facilitates metalinguistic processing which eventually leads to what is often called metalinguistic awareness, metalinguistic knowledge, or metalinguistic ability. . . , a skill that good language learners seem to possess or acquire without difficulty." See Schneider, *Multisensory*, 62 (see chap. 1, n. 3).

10. Leonore Ganschow and Richard L. Sparks, "Reflections on Foreign Language Study for Students with Language Learning Problems: Research, Issues, and Challenges," *Dyslexia* 6 (2000): 87–100.

11. Suzanne Graham, "A Study of Students' Metacognitive Beliefs about Foreign Language Study and Their Impact on Learning," *Foreign Language Annals* 39 (2006): 297.

12. Jennifer A. Livingston, "Metacognition: An Overview," ERIC, 2003, http://search .proquest.com.lib-proxy.calvin.edu/docview/62223833?accountid=9844.

13. Francisco, "Learning Disabilities," 6 (see intro., n. 6).

14. Barry J. Zimmerman and Albert Bandura, "Impact of Self-Regulatory Influences on Writing Course Attainment," *American Educational Research Journal* 31, no. 4 (1994): 848.

15. My students averaged in the 20.6th/18th percentile on the two parts of the Modern Language Aptitude Test (MLAT—long version). The fifteen males averaged in the 16.2th/20.5th percentile, and the fourteen females in the 20th/20.6th percentile. The students in the modified foreign-language program at the University of Colorado at Boulder generally score below the tenth percentile overall. (See Doris M. Downey and Lynn E. Snyder, "Curricular Accommodations for College Students with Language Learning Disabilities," *Topics in Language Disorders* 21, no. 2 [2001]: 64.) My students included one male and five female sophomores, seven female and eight male juniors, and two female and six male seniors. Majors were business (six), social work (four), psychology (three), education (three), communication/media studies (three), and exercise science (two), and there was one student each in biology/premed, economics, history, political science, rhetoric, interdisciplinary, fine art, and unknown.

16. Edward A. Polloway and Tom E. C. Smith, *Language Instruction for Students with Disabilities* (Denver, CO: Love, 2000), 359.

17. Parker J. Palmer, *The Courage to Teach: Exploring the Inner Landscape of a Teacher's Life* (San Francisco: Jossey-Bass, 1998), 128.

18. Leonore Ganschow, Jenafer Lloyd-Jones, and Thomas R. Miles, "Dyslexia and Musical Notation," *Annals of Dyslexia* 44 (1994): 185–203; Gardner, *Intelligence Reframed*, 31–105 (see ch. 1, n. 3); Overy, "Dyslexia and Music," 497–505 (see chap. 1, n. 3); Johansson, "Cultural and Linguistic Influence," 13–50 (see chap. 1, n. 4).

19. Overy, "Dyslexia and Music," 503 (see chap. 1, n. 3).

20. Johansson, "Cultural and Linguistic Influence," 37, 39 (see chap. 1, n. 4); Gardner, *Intelligence Reframed*, 42 (see chap. 1, n. 3).

21. James Bradley prompted me to think about the concept of intentional forgiveness by students who have had prior negative classroom experiences so that they can become successful foreign-language learners. This story is developed in David I. Smith, "On Viewing Learners as Spiritual Beings: Implications for Language Educators," *Journal of Christianity and Foreign Languages* 9 (2008): 34–48; and in David I. Smith, John Shortt, and James Bradley, "Reconciliation in the Classroom," *Journal of Education and Christian Belief* 10, no. 1 (2006): 3–5.

22. From Thomas R. Miles, *Dyslexia: The Pattern of Difficulties*, quoted in Dominic Griffiths and Melanie Hardman, "Specific Learning Difficulties (Dyslexia) and Modern Foreign Languages," *Language Learning Journal* 10 (1994): 84.

23. Sparks, Schneider, and Ganschow, "Teaching Foreign (Second) Language," 55–83 (see intro., n. 6).

24. Nancy Pompian, "Like a Volvo off My Chest," *The Undergraduate Bulletin: Dartmouth College* 5, no. 1 (1986): 1–2.

25. Miles, quoted in Griffiths and Hardman, 84 (see chap. 3, n. 22).

26. Lisa Belkin, "Office Messes," *New York Times Magazine*, July 18, 2004, http://www .nytimes.com/2004/07/18/magazine/office-messes.html.

27. Katy Human, "Making Sense of the Senses," *Denver Post*, July 22, 2007, http://www.denverpost.com/search/ci_6433995.

28. Lidy M. Pelsser, Jan K. Buitelaar, and Huub F. Savelkoul, "ADHD as a (Non) Allergic Hypersensitivity Disorder: A Hypothesis," *Pediatric Allergy and Immunology* 20, no. 2 (2009): 299–300.

29. Miles, quoted in Griffiths and Hardman, 84 (see chap. 3, n. 22).

30. Terrence Sejnowski, "Sleep and Memory," *Current Biology* 5, no. 8 (1995): 832–34; Elisabet Service, "Phonology, Working Memory, and Foreign Language Learning," *Quarterly Journal of Experimental Psychology* 45A (1992): 21–50; David N. Neubauer, "Sleep and Memory," *Primary Psychiatry* 16, no. 8 (2009): 19–21.

31. Robertson, "Neuropsychology," 202–10 (see intro., n. 3).

32. Polloway and Smith, "Handwriting Instruction," in *Language Instruction for Students with Disabilities,* 368 (see chap. 3, n. 16).

33. Ibid.," 369 (see chap. 3, n. 16); Mark J. Penn and E. Kenney Zalesne, *Microtrends: The Small Forces behind Tomorrow's Big Changes* (New York: Twelve, 2009), 89.

34. Daniel C. Richardson and Michael J. Spivey, "Eye Tracking: Research Areas and Applications," in *Encyclopedia of Biomaterials and Biomedical Engineering*, ed. Gary L. Bowlin and Gary Wnek (New York: Marcel Dekker, 2004), 1033–43.

35. Susan Rvachew et al., "The Impact of Early Onset Otitis Media on Babbling and Early Language Development," *Journal of the Acoustical Society of America* 105, no. 1 (1999): 468.

36. Miles, quoted in Griffiths and Hardman, 84 (see ch. 3, n. 22).

37. "Meet the Experts: Dr. Maryanne Wolf (Teachers)," YouTube, May 19, 2008, http://www.youtube.com/watch?v=KsqpXyPC-II.

38. Sparks et al., "Native Language Predictors," 129–60 (see intro., n. 6).

39. Mitchell Rosenthal et al., *Rehabilitation of the Adult and Child with Traumatic Brain Injury*, 3rd ed. (Philadelphia: F. A. Davis, 1999), 77–84.

40. Levine, *Mind at a Time*, 265 (see ch. 1, n. 9).

41. Ibid., 266.

Chapter 4: Using Journals to Help Students Learn How to Learn

1. Christine Goh, "Metacognitive Awareness and Second Language Listeners," *ELT Journal* 51 (1997): 368; Eve Leons, Christie Herbert, and Ken Gobbo, "Students with Learning Disabilities and Ad/Hd in the Foreign Language Classroom: Supporting Students and Instructors," *Foreign Language Annals* 42, no. 1 (2009): 47.

2. Wenden, "Metacognitive Knowledge," 530–31 (see chap. 3, n. 7).

3. Paris and Winograd, "How Metacognition Can Promote," 31 (see chap. 3, n. 4).

4. Carissa Young and Fong Yoke Sim, "Learner Diaries as a Tool to Heighten Chinese Students' Metacognitive Awareness of English Learning," in *Teaching English to Students from China*, ed. Gek Ling Lee (Singapore: Singapore University Press, 2003), 31.

5. Stephen D. Krashen, *The Input Hypothesis: Issues and Implications* (New York: Longman, 1985), 3.

Chapter 5: Teaching Directly and Explicitly to Maximize Student Learning

1. McIntyre and Pickering, "Multisensory Structured Language Programs," http://www.ldonline.org/article/6332 (see chap. 1, n. 2); Leonore Ganschow and Elke Schneider, "Assisting Students with Foreign Language Learning Difficulties in School," LD Online, 2006, http://www.ldonline.org/article/Assisting_Students_with_Foreign_Language_Learning_Difficulties_in_School.

2. Winograd and Hare, "Direct Instruction," 121–39 (see chap. 2, n. 7). They cite Barak V. Rosenshine, "Teaching Functions in Instructional Programs," *The Elementary School Journal* 83 (1983): 335–51.

3. Sparks and Ganschow, "Foreign Language Learning Differences," 3–16 (see intro., n. 8).

4. Leonore Ganschow, Richard L. Sparks, and James Javorsky, "Foreign Language Learning Difficulties: An Historical Perspective," *Journal of Learning Disabilities* 31, no. 3 (1998): 248–58. doi:10.1177/002221949803100304.

5. Ganschow and Sparks, "Reflections on Foreign Language Study," 87–100 (see chap. 3, n. 10); Sparks, Schneider, and Ganschow, "Teaching Foreign (Second) Language," 67, 69 (see intro., n. 6).

6. Charlann S. Simon, "Dyslexia and Learning a Foreign Language: A Personal Experience," *Annals of Dyslexia* 50 (2000): 155–87.

7. "The teaching of phonology/orthography, syntax, and semantics will differ depending on the language. French, for instance, may require more focus on pronunciation and spelling than Spanish because of its many silent letters and unfamiliar sounds for native speakers of English. See Sparks, Schneider, and Ganschow, "Teaching Foreign (Second) Language," 70 (see intro., n. 6).

8. Sparks, Schneider, and Ganschow, "Teaching Foreign (Second) Language," 70 (see intro., n. 6).

9. Ibid.

10. Thanks to Amanda Boes for this idea.

11. Sparks, et al., "Native Language Predictors," 132, 153 (see intro., n. 6). Also see Service, "Phonology," 21–50 (see chap. 3, n. 30); Leonore Ganschow and Richard L. Sparks, "Effects of Direct Instruction in Spanish Phonology on the Native Language Skills and Foreign Language Aptitude of At-Risk Foreign Language Learners," *Journal of Learning Disabilities* 28, no. 2 (1995): 107–20; McIntyre and Pickering, "Multisensory Structured Language Programs," http://www.ldonline.org/article/6332 (see chap. 1, n. 2); Schneider, "Foreign Language Learning," (see intro., n. 7); Schneider, *Multisensory* (chap. 1, n. 3); Margaret A. Crombie, "Dyslexia and the Learning of a Foreign Language in School: Where Are We Going?" *Dyslexia* 6 (2000): 112–23; Downey and Snyder, "Curricular Accommodations," 55–67 (see chap. 3, n. 15); Grigorenko, "Foreign Language Acquisition," 95–112 (see intro., n. 10); and Irene Brouwer Konyndyk, "Multisensory Structured Metacognitive Foreign Language: A Solution for Students with Learning Disabilities" (paper presented at the Second International Conference on New Directions in the Humanities, Prato, Italy, 2004).

12. Sparks, Schneider, and Ganschow, "Teaching Foreign (Second) Language," 64, 69 (see intro., n. 6); Schneider, *Multisensory*, 65 (see chap. 1, n. 3).

13. In France, a week is considered to have eight days ("in a week" is translated *dans huit jours*). Perhaps the etymological origin of the word is rooted in "to the day of eight."

14. Schneider, *Multisensory*, 65 (see chap. 1, n. 3).

15. The well-known phrase *s'il vous plaît* is generally translated as "please" but literally means "if it you pleases" (i.e., "if it is pleasing to you"). By examining the smaller morphemes, students can use those pieces to build new phrases, such as *s'il te plaît* (the informal version of "please") or *Ça me plaît* ("That pleases me," which is generally translated as "I like that"). Amanda Boes tells her students that *il y a* ("there is/there are") literally means "he has there"; she has students make goofy sentences with the phrase to quickly catch its meaning.

16. Helping students learn literal meanings of morphemes is also useful when learning reflexive/pronominal verbs. For example, *se lever* literally means "to get oneself up" and *s'appeler* literally means "to call oneself," even though this is usually translated "to be called."

17. Many of my students do poorly on the 24 percent of the Modern Language Aptitude Test that addresses this area of language aptitude; this section (IV) tests a student's sensitivity to grammatical aspects of language, and how words function in sentences.

18. Deborah Blaz, *Foreign Language Teacher's Guide to Active Learning* (Larchmont, NY: Eye on Education, 1999), 125.

19. In *C'est*, the *e* of *Ce* dropped due to the elision of two vowels when the first vowel is an unstressed schwa sound.

20. Other examples in Spanish are *desgracia,* which means "misfortune," and *decepción,* which means "disappointment." In French, *déception* means "disappointment."

21. See Laura K. Lawless, "French Words and Expressions in English," About.com website, n.d., http://french.about.com/library/bl-frenchinenglish-list.htm?p=1.

22. These easily recognizable words come from a variety of social arenas such as dance (*ballet, grand jeté, plié, barre*); food and the culinary arts (*sous-chef, sauté, sorbet, flambé, soufflé,*

hors d'oeuvre, croissant); government (*laissez-faire, coup d'état, détente, chargé d'affaires*); the military (*espionage, sabotage, sortie*); business (*entrepreneur*); literature (*roman à clef, nom de plume, mot juste*); philosophy (*raison d'être*); the fine life (*connoisseur, joie de vivre, RSVP, rendez-vous, pied à terre, débutante*); the fine arts (*oeuvre d'art, film noir, art nouveau*); visual art (*plein air painting, trompe l'oeil*); fencing (*en garde, touché*); fashion (*haute couture, négligée, décolletage, chic*); and sports (*l'oeuf* — "the egg"—which evolved into the tennis term "love"); and other miscellaneous phrases (*faux pas, entre nous, fait accompli, double entendre*).

23. One word that English speakers have borrowed from French, and which they both mispronounce and misspell, is "chaise lounge" (referring to a chair in which to lounge); the phrase in French, however, is *chaise longue,* which means "LONG chair."

24. Likewise, in the two major past tenses in French (*Passé Composé* and *Imparfait*), two of the three translations of the verbs are quite different in English: in the *Passé Composé, j'ai chanté* = I sang; I did sing; I have sung (here "I have sung" looks most like the French equivalent); in the *Imparfait, je chantais* = I sang; I was singing; I used to sing (here "I sang" looks most like the French equivalent). Explicitly teaching the translation of these different forms helps students understand how they can be used differently. Both can mean "I sang," but when you want to give the impression of a completed past action, you say "I have sung" or "I did sing." And if you want to give the impression of a repeated or habitual past action, you say "I was singing" or "I used to sing" and thus use the *Imparfait* in French.

25. If my students have already learned past tenses, I ask them to predict what the past participle of the verb might be, and whether it is conjugated with *être* or *avoir* in the *Passé Composé* tense. I remind them that this is a "comings/goings" verb, so I expect they'll tell me that it is conjugated with *être*. We also discuss agreement on the past participle. Then I have them write out the "I" form in the *Imparfait* tense.

26. Another example is teaching how to form reflexive verbs. I have students write on the whiteboard *je me lève* = "I get myself up" and then ask them to predict how the *tu* form might look. I expect them to write *tu te* lèves, etc.

27. DR. and MRS. VANDER TRAMP
Devenir; Revenir; Monter; Retourner; Sortir
Venir; Aller; Naître; Descendre; Entrer; Rester
Tomber; Rentrer; Arriver; Mourir; Partir (pronominals)

Since my students never learn this entire list, we have redone the list into a different acronym— MAD TRRAPPERS—to include the verbs they've learned. It includes *Monter, Aller, Descendre, Tomber, Rentrer, Retourner, Arriver, Pronominals/Reflexives, Partir, Entrer, Rester, Sortir.* Later the verb *venir* is also added. This acronym gives students a chance to work on rolling their French r to say the acronym.

28. *Estoy* ("I am"), *estás* ("you—familiar singular—are"), *está* ("he, she, it is"), *estamos* ("we are"), *estáis* ("you—familiar plural—are"), *están* ("you—formal—are; they are"). Thanks to Becky Kissinger for the idea.

29. Thanks to Renee Roodvoets for this idea. This Addams Family melody could also be used in French, as follows: *Chantons les jours!* (Snap! Snap!) *Chantons les jours!* (Snap! Snap!) *Chantons les jours! Chantons les jours! de la semaine!* (Snap! Snap!) *Le lundi et le mardi, le mercredi, le jeudi, le vendredi, le samedi, et le dimanche!* (Snap! Snap!) It would be more culturally authentic to use a real French melody.

30. I thank my daughter Liesje Konyndyk-O'Farrell for this song.

31. Thanks to Kara Feikema for this idea.

32. With the *Imparfait* tense, *ais* is often written *ias*. I tell them that *ias* doesn't exist in French and that alphabetically the *a* will come before the *i*.

Chapter 6: Serving Students with Best Practices

1. Marjorie Hall Haley, e-mail with author, May 30, 2000.

2. Downey and Snyder, "Curricular Accommodations," 55–67 (see chap. 3, n. 15).

3. Ibid., 61 (see chap. 3, n. 15).

4. In Spanish, these verbs would be *estar* ("to be"), *ser* ("to be"), *tener* ("to have"), *ir* ("to go"), and *hacer* ("to do/make"). In German, they would be *sein* ("to be"), *haben* ("to have"), *gehen* ("to go"), and *machen* ("to make/do").

5. In Spanish, these verbs would be *-ar* (e.g., *hablar*—"to speak"), *-er* (e.g., *comer*—"to eat"), and *-ir* (e.g., *vivir*—"to live").

6. Downey and Snyder, "Curricular Accommodations," 62 (see chap. 3, n. 15); Arries, "Learning Disabilities," 198 (see intro., n. 7).

7. Paris and Winograd, "How Metacognition Can Promote," 40 (see chap. 3, n. 4).

8. Margaret Crombie and Hilary McColl, "Teaching Modern Foreign Languages to Dyslexic Learners: A Scottish Perspective," in *Multilingualism, Literacy, and Dyslexia: A Challenge for Educators*, ed. Lindsay Peer and Gavin Reid (London: David Fulton, 2000), 216.

9. Downey and Snyder, "Curricular Accommodations," 62 (see chap. 3, n. 15).

10. Francisco, "Learning Disabilities," 5 (see intro., n. 6).

11. Paris and Winograd, "How Metacognition Can Promote," 40 (see chap. 3, n. 4).

12. Arries, "Learning Disabilities," 106 (see intro., n. 7).

13. I'm grateful to Cindy Klaver for this concept.

14. Palmer, *Courage to Teach*, 89, 115 (see chap. 3, n. 17).

15. DiFino and Lombardino, "Language Learning Disabilities," 390–400 (see intro., n. 2).

16. The handout from the modified foreign-language program at the University of Colorado at Boulder describes tendencies that could signal difficulties in the area of performance, learning/study habits, and attitude.

17. Downey and Snyder, "Curricular Accommodations," 60–61 (see chap. 3, n. 15).

18. Ibid., 62 (see chap. 3, n. 15).

19. Winograd and Hare, "Direct Instruction," 122 (see chap. 2, n. 7).

20. Levine, *Mind at a Time*, 73 (see chap. 1, n. 9).

21. In French, one uses the "Gallic pout" to produce the *u* sound, which doesn't exist in English; you need to pucker up your lips and say "ee."

22. Thanks to Kara Feikema for this idea. It goes like this:
Lunes, martes; lunes, martes ("Monday, Tuesday; Monday, Tuesday");
Miércoles; miércoles ("Wednesday; Wednesday");
Jueves, viernes, sábado; jueves, viernes, sábado ("Thursday, Friday, Saturday; Thursday, Friday, Saturday");
Domingo; domingo ("Sunday; Sunday").

23. Cindy Klaver, who shared this idea, gets background music from the "Art of Glow" app.

24. This construction is used in Spanish to express what someone likes, e.g., *Me gusta el chocolate* means "I like chocolate" but literally means "Chocolate is pleasing to me." Similarly *Me gustan las manzanas* means "I like apples" or "Apples are pleasing to me." Other verbs she uses are *encantar* ("to charm"), *faltar* ("to be lacking/missing"), *quedar* ("to be left over"), *doler* ("to hurt; to cause pain"), *parecer* ("to seem/appear; to resemble"), and *aburrir* ("to bore; to vex").

25. The other four Cs are communication, connections, comparisons, and communities. "National Standards for Foreign Language Education," American Council on the Teaching of Foreign Languages website, n.d., http://www.actfl.org/i4a/pages/index.cfm?pageid=3392.

26. H. Ned Seelye, *Teaching Culture: Strategies for Intercultural Communication*, 3rd ed. (Lincolnwood, IL: National Textbook Company, 1993).

27. An excellent resource is David I. Smith and Barbara Carvill, *The Gift of the Stranger: Faith, Hospitality, and Foreign Language Learning* (Grand Rapids, MI: Eerdmans, 2000). I use part of the following book for a student reflective journal entry, requiring students to read chapter 6 and write two paragraphs—a summary and a reaction to the chapter: David I. Smith, *Learning from the Stranger: Christian Faith and Cultural Diversity* (Grand Rapids, MI: Eerdmans, 2009).

28. I put these books on reserve in our school library: Ross Steele, *When in France, Do as the French Do: The Clued-In Guide to French Life, Language, and Culture* (Chicago, IL: McGraw-Hill, 2002); Jean-Benoit Nadeau and Julie Barlow, *Sixty Million Frenchmen Can't Be Wrong: Why We Love France but Not the French* (Naperville, IL: Sourcebooks, 2003); and Polly Platt, *French or Foe? Getting the Most out of Visiting, Living, and Working in France* (London: Culture Crossing, 2003). (The book is distributed in the US by Distribooks, based in Skokie, Illinois).

Chapter 7: Equipping Students to Learn Responsibly

1. I thank Marcie Pyper for this metaphor.

2. Paris and Winograd, "How Metacognition Can Promote," 30 (see chap. 3, n. 4).

3. Jere Brophy, "Failure Syndrome Students," *ERIC Digest Report* No. EDO-PS-98-2 (Champaign, IL: ERIC Clearinghouse on Elementary and Early Childhood Education, 1998).

4. Andrew D. Cohen, *Language Learning Insights for Learners, Teachers, and Researchers* (New York: Newbury House, 1990), 192.

5. Winograd and Hare, "Direct Instruction," 122 (see chap. 2, n. 7).

6. Parker J. Palmer, "Teaching with Heart and Soul: Reflections on Spirituality in Teacher Education," *Journal of Teacher Education* 54 (November/December 2003): 376–85.

7. While it is wonderful to add *hier soir* ("last night") to the sentence, it's not vital to the formation of a complete sentence. If the student is uncertain about spelling, it would probably be better to omit the phrase completely.

8. Many researchers recommend immediate feedback. For instance, see Downey and Snyder, "College Students," 82–92 (see chap. 1, n. 3).

9. Nicole Mills, Frank Pajares, and Carol Herron, "Self-Efficacy of College Intermediate French Students: Relation to Achievement and Motivation," *Language Learning* 57, no. 3 (2007): 417–18).

10. Winograd and Hare, "Direct Instruction," 122 (see chap. 2, n. 7).

11. Leons, Herbert, and Gobbo, "Students with Learning Disabilities," 47 (see chap. 4, n. 1).

12. Arries, "Learning Disabilities," 106 (see intro., n. 7).

13. Downey and Snyder, "Curricular Accommodations," 62 (see chap. 3, n. 15).

14. Scholars recommend visual organizers to help English as a Second Language students. See Robin L. Schwarz, "Identifying and Helping Learning-Disabled English as a Second Language (ESL) Students in a College Intensive English Programme," in *Multilingualism, Literacy, and Dyslexia: A Challenge for Educators*, ed. Lindsay Peer and Gavin Reid (London: David Fulton, 2000), 197.

15. This is strongly recommended by Downey and Snyder, "Curricular Accommodations," 62 (see chap. 3, n. 15).

Bibliography

Ackerman, Diane A. *A Natural History of the Senses.* New York: Vintage Books, 1990.

Amend, Amanda E., Carolyn A. Whitney, Antonia T. Messuri, and Hideko Furukawa. "A Modified Spanish Sequence for Students with Language-Based Learning Disabilities." *Foreign Language Annals* 42, no. 1 (2009): 27–41.

Arries, Jonathan F. "Learning Disabilities and Foreign Languages: A Curriculum Approach to the Design of Inclusive Courses." *Modern Language Journal* 83 (1999): 98–110.

Aud, Susan, William Hussar, Michael Planty, Thomas Snyder, Kevin Bianco, Mary Ann Fox, Lauren Frohlich, Jana Kemp, and Lauren Drake, "Participation in Education," in *The Condition of Education 2010,* sec. 1. Washington, DC: National Center for Education Statistics, Institute of Education Sciences, US Department of Education, 2010.

Blaz, Deborah. *Foreign Language Teacher's Guide to Active Learning.* Larchmont, NY: Eye on Education, 1999.

Brophy, Jere. "Failure Syndrome Students," *ERIC Digest Report* No. EDO-PS-98-2. Champaign, IL: ERIC Clearinghouse on Elementary and Early Childhood Education, 1998.

Chamot, Anna U. "The Learning Strategies of ESL Students." In *Learner Strategies in Language Learning,* edited by Anita Wenden and J. Rubin, 71–83. London: Prentice-Hall, 1987.

Cohen, Andrew D. *Language Learning Insights for Learners, Teachers, and Researchers.* New York: Newbury House, 1990.

Crombie, Margaret A. "Dyslexia and the Learning of a Foreign Language in School: Where Are We Going?" *Dyslexia* 6 (2000): 112–23.

———. "The Effects of Specific Learning Difficulties (Dyslexia) on the Learning of Foreign Language in School." *Dyslexia* 3 (1997): 27–47.

Crombie, Margaret, and Hilary McColl. "Teaching Modern Foreign Languages to Dyslexic Learners: A Scottish Perspective." In *Multilingualism, Literacy, and Dyslexia: A Challenge for Educators,* edited by Lindsay Peer and Gavin Reid, 211–17. London: David Fulton, 2000.

DiFino, Sharon M., and Linda J. Lombardino. "Language Learning Disabilities: The Ultimate Foreign Language Challenge." *Foreign Language Annals* 37 (2004): 390–400.

Dinklage, Kenneth T. "The Inability to Learn a Foreign Language." In *Emotional Problems of the Student,* edited by Graham Blaine and Charles MacArthur, 185–206. New York: Appleton-Century-Crofts, 1971.

Downey, Doris M., and Lynn E. Snyder. "College Students with Learning Language–Learning Disorders: The Phonological Core as Risk for Failure in Foreign Language Classes." *Topics in Language Disorders* 21, no. 1 (2000): 82–92.

———. "Curricular Accommodations for College Students with Language Learning Disabilities." *Topics in Language Disorders* 21, no. 2 (2001): 55–67.

Dreifus, Claudia. "The Sweet Smell of Success." *AARP Bulletin,* October 2005, 26–27.

Ehrman, Madeline. "The Modern Language Aptitude Test for Predicting Learning Success and Advising Students." *Applied Language Learning* 9, nos. 1 and 2 (1998): 31–70.

Flavell, John H. "Metacognition and Cognitive Monitoring: A New Area of Cognitive-Developmental Inquiry." *American Psychologist* 34, no. 10 (1979): 906–11.

Francisco, Dorcas. "Learning Disabilities and the Foreign Language Classroom." *Language Resource Newsletter,* 2005, 5–8.

Gajar, Anna H. "Foreign Language Learning Disabilities: The Identification of Predictive and Diagnostic Variables." *Journal of Learning Disabilities* 20, no. 6 (1987): 327–30.

Ganschow, Leonore, Jenafer Lloyd-Jones, and Thomas R. Miles. "Dyslexia and Musical Notation." *Annals of Dyslexia* 44 (1994): 185–203.

Ganschow, Leonore, and Richard L. Sparks. "Effects of Direct Instruction in Spanish Phonology on the Native Language Skills and Foreign Language Aptitude of At-Risk Foreign Language Learners." *Journal of Learning Disabilities* 28, no. 2 (1995): 107–20.

———. "'Foreign' Language Learning Disabilities: Issues, Research, and Teaching Implications." In *Success for College Students with Learning Disabilities*, edited by S. Vogel and Pamela Adelman, 283–320. New York: Springer, 1993.

———. "Reflections on Foreign Language Study for Students with Language Learning Problems: Research, Issues, and Challenges." *Dyslexia* 6 (2000): 87–100.

Ganschow, Leonore, Richard L. Sparks, and James Javorsky. "Foreign Language Learning Difficulties: An Historical Perspective. *Journal of Learning Disabilities* 31, no. 3 (1998): 248–58. doi:10.1177/002221949803100304.

Gardner, Howard. *Intelligence Reframed: Multiple Intelligences for the 21st Century*. New York: Basic Books, 1999.

———. *Multiple Intelligences: The Theory in Practice*. New York: Basic Books, 1993.

Goh, Christine. "Metacognitive Awareness and Second Language Listeners." *ELT Journal* 51 (1997): 361–69.

Graham, Suzanne. "Learners' Metacognitive Beliefs: A Modern Foreign Languages Case Study." *Research in Education* 70, no. 2 (2003): 9–20.

———. "A Study of Students' Metacognitive Beliefs about Foreign Language Study and Their Impact on Learning." *Foreign Language Annals* 39 (2006): 296–309.

Griffiths, Dominic, and Melanie Hardman. "Specific Learning Difficulties (Dyslexia) and Modern Foreign Languages." *Language Learning Journal* 10 (1994): 84–85.

Grigorenko, Elena L. "Foreign Language Acquisition and Language-Based Learning Disabilities." In *Individual Differences and Instructed Language Learning*, edited by Peter Robinson, 95–112. Amsterdam: John Benjamins, 2002.

Ho, Yim-Chi, Cheung Mei-Chun, and Agnes S. Chan. "Music Training Improves Verbal but Not Visual Memory: Cross-Sectional and Longitudinal Explorations in Children." *Neuropsychology* 17, no. 3 (2003): 439–50.

Horwitz, Elaine K. "The Beliefs about Language Learning of Beginning University Foreign Language Students." *Modern Language Journal* 72 (1988): 28–94.

Johansson, Barbro B. "Cultural and Linguistic Influence on Brain Organization for Language and Possible Consequences for Dyslexia: A Review." *Annals of Dyslexia* 56 (2006): 13–50.

Kilgour, Andrea R., Lorna S. Jakobson, and Lola L. Cuddy. "Music Training and Rate of Presentation as Mediator of Text and Song Recall." *Memory and Cognition* 28 (2000): 700–710.

Koelsch, Stefan, Elizabeth Kasper, Daniela Sammler, Katrin Schulze, Thomas Gunter, and Angela D. Friederici. "Music, Language, and Meaning: Brain Signatures of Semantic Processing." *Nature Neuroscience* 7 (2004): 302–7.

Konyndyk, Irene Brouwer. "Direct and Explicit Instruction in the Foreign Language Classroom: Showing Hospitality to Students with Learning Disabilities." *Journal of Christianity and Foreign Languages* 12 (2011): 79–85.

———. "Multisensory Structured Metacognitive Foreign Language: A Solution for Students with Learning Disabilities." Paper presented at the Second International Conference on New Directions in the Humanities, Prato, Italy, July 2004.

———. "Teaching French (and Spanish) to Students with Dyslexia: Comparative Perspectives." Paper presented at the International Dyslexia Association Conference, Washington, DC, June 2002.

Krashen, Stephen D. *The Input Hypothesis: Issues and Implications*. New York: Longman, 1985.

Leons, Eve, Christie Herbert, and Ken Gobbo. "Students with Learning Disabilities and Ad/Hd in the Foreign Language Classroom: Supporting Students and Instructors," *Foreign Language Annals* 42, no. 1 (2009): 42–54.

Levine, Mel. *A Mind at a Time*. New York: Simon and Schuster, 2002.

Maess, Burkhard, Stefan Koelsch, Thomas Gunter, and Angela D. Friederici. "Musical Syntax Is Processed in Broca's Area: An MEG Study." *Nature Neuroscience* 4 (2001): 540–45.

Miles, Thomas R. *Dyslexia: The Pattern of Difficulties*. Springfield, IL: Thomas, 1983.

Mills, Nicole, Frank Pajares, and Carol Herron. "Self-Efficacy of College Intermediate French Students: Relation to Achievement and Motivation." *Language Learning* 57, no. 3 (2007): 417–18.

Morris, Edwin T. "The Importance of Olfaction, Key Sense in Scent." In *Fragrance: The Story of Perfume from Cleopatra to Chanel*, 35–52. New York: Charles Scribner's Sons, 1984.

Nadeau, Jean-Benoit, and Julie Barlow. *Sixty Million Frenchmen Can't Be Wrong: Why We Love France but Not the French*. Naperville, IL: Sourcebooks, 2003.

Neubauer, David N. "Sleep and Memory." *Primary Psychiatry* 16, no. 8 (2009): 19–21.

Nouwen, Henri J. *Reaching Out: The Three Movements of the Spiritual Life*. Garden City, NY: Image Books, 1986.

Overy, Katie. "Dyslexia and Music: From Timing Deficits to Musical Intervention." *Annals of the New York Academy of Sciences* 999 (2003): 497–505.

Oxford, Rebecca. "Styles, Strategies, and Aptitude: Connections for Languages in the United States." In *Language Aptitude Reconsidered*, edited by Thomas Parry and Charles Stansfield, 67–125. Englewood Cliffs, NJ: Prentice Hall, 2005.

Palmer, Douglas J., and Ernest T. Goetz. "Selection and Use of Study Strategies: The Role of the Studier's Beliefs about Self and Strategies." In *Learning and Study Strategies: Issues in Assessment, Instruction, and Evaluation*, edited by Claire E. Weinstein, Ernest T. Goetz, and Patricia A. Alexander, 41–61. Gainesville, FL: Florida Academic Press, 1988.

Palmer, Parker J. *The Courage to Teach: Exploring the Inner Landscape of a Teacher's Life*. San Francisco: Jossey-Bass, 1998.

———. "Teaching with Heart and Soul: Reflections on Spirituality in Teacher Education." *Journal of Teacher Education* 54 (November/December 2003): 376–85.

———. *To Know as We Are Known: Education as a Spiritual Journey*. San Francisco: Harper & Row, 1983.

Paris, Scott G., and Peter Winograd. "How Metacognition Can Promote Academic Learning and Instruction." In *Dimension of Thinking and Cognitive Instruction*, edited by Beau Fly Jones and Lorna Idol, 15–51. Hillsdale, NJ: Erlbaum, 1990.

Pelsser, Lidy M., Jan K. Buitelaar, and Huub F. Savelkoul. "ADHD as a (Non) Allergic Hypersensitivity Disorder: A Hypothesis." *Pediatric Allergy and Immunology* 20, no. 2 (2009): 299–300.

Penn, Mark J., and E. Kenney Zalesne. *Microtrends: The Small Forces behind Tomorrow's Big Changes*. New York: Twelve, 2009.

Pimsleur, Paul, Donald Sundland, and Ruth McIntyre. "Underachievement in Foreign Language Learning." *International Review of Applied Linguistics* 2 (1964): 113–50.

Platt, Polly. *French or Foe? Getting the Most out of Visiting, Living, and Working in France*. London: Culture Crossing, 2003.

Polloway, Edward A., and Tom E. C. Smith. *Language Instruction for Students with Disabilities*. Denver, CO: Love, 2000.

Pompian, Nancy. "Like a Volvo off My Chest." *The Undergraduate Bulletin: Dartmouth College* 5, no. 1 (1986): 1–2.

Richardson, Daniel C., and Michael J. Spivey. "Eye Tracking: Research Areas and Applications." In *Encyclopedia of Biomaterials and Biomedical Engineering*, edited by Gary L. Bowlin and Gary Wnek, 573–82. New York: Marcel Dekker, 2004.

Robertson, Jean. "The Neuropsychology of Modern Foreign Language Learning." In *Multilingualism, Literacy and Dyslexia: A Challenge for Educators*, edited by Lindsay Peer and Gavin Reid, 202–10. London: David Fulton, 2000.

Rosenshine, Barak V. "Teaching Functions in Instructional Programs." *The Elementary School Journal* 83 (1983): 335–51.

Rosenthal, Mitchell, Ernest R. Griffith, Jeffrey S. Kreutzer, and Brian Pentland. *Rehabilitation of the Adult and Child with Traumatic Brain Injury*. 3rd ed. Philadelphia: F. A. Davis, 1999.

Rvachew, Susan, Elzbieta B. Slawinski, Megan Williams, and Carol L. Green. "The Impact of Early Onset Otitis Media on Babbling and Early Language Development." *Journal of the Acoustical Society of America* 105, no. 1 (1999): 468.

Sacks, Oliver. "When Music Heals." *Parade*, March 31, 2002, 4–5.

Schneider, Elke. "Foreign Language Learning and Learning Disabilities: Instructional Alternatives." Workshop presented at the Foreign Language Forum of Calvin College, Grand
   Rapids, MI, October 1998.

———. *Multisensory Structured Metacognitive Instruction: An Approach to Teaching a Foreign
   Language to At-Risk Students.* Hamburg, Germany: Peter Lang, 1999.

Schön, Danielle, Cyrille Magne, and Mireille Besson. "The Music of Speech: Music Training
   Facilitates Pitch Processing in Both Music and Language." *Psychophysiology* 41 (2004):
   34–49.

Schwarz, Robin L. "Identifying and Helping Learning-Disabled English as a Second Language
   (ESL) Students in a College Intensive English Programme." In *Multilingualism, Literacy,
   and Dyslexia: A Challenge for Educators*, edited by Lindsay Peer and Gavin Reid, 192–202.
   London: David Fulton, 2000.

Seelye, H. Ned. *Teaching Culture: Strategies for Intercultural Communication.* 3rd ed. Lincolnwood, IL: National Textbook Company, 1993.

Sejnowski, Terrence. "Sleep and Memory." *Current Biology* 5, no. 8 (1995): 832–34.

Service, Elisabet. "Phonology, Working Memory, and Foreign Language Learning." *Quarterly
   Journal of Experimental Psychology* 45A (1992): 21–50.

Sheffield, Betty B. "The Structured Flexibility of Orton-Gillingham." *Annals of Dyslexia* 41 (1991):
   41–54.

Shrum, Judith L., and Elaine W. Glisan. *Teacher's Handbook: Contextualized Language Instruction.* Boston: Heinle & Heinle, 1994.

Simon, Charlann S. "Dyslexia and Learning a Foreign Language: A Personal Experience."
   Annals of Dyslexia 50 (2000): 155–87.

Smith, David I. *Learning from the Stranger: Christian Faith and Cultural Diversity.* Grand Rapids,
   MI: Eerdmans , 2009.

———. "On Viewing Learners as Spiritual Beings: Implications for Language Educators." *Journal of Christianity and Foreign Languages* 9 (2008): 34–48.

Smith, David I., and Barbara Carvill. *The Gift of the Stranger: Faith, Hospitality, and Foreign Language Learning.* Grand Rapids, MI: Eerdmans, 2000.

Smith, David I., John Shortt, and James Bradley. "Reconciliation in the Classroom." *Journal of
   Education and Christian Belief* 10, no. 1 (2006): 3–5.

Sparks, Richard L. "At-Risk Second Language Learners: Problems, Solutions, and Challenges."
   Foreign Language Annals 42 (2009): 4.

———. "Foreign Language Learning Problems of Students Classified as Learning-Disabled
   and Non-Learning Disabled: Is There a Difference?" *Topics in Language Disorders* 21, no. 2
   (2001): 38–54.

———. "Intelligence, Learning Disabilities, Attention Deficit Hyperactivity Disorder, and Foreign Language Learning Problems: A Research Update." *ADFL Bulletin* 36, no. 2 (2005):
   43–50.

Sparks, Richard L., and Leonore Ganschow. "Foreign Language Learning Differences: Affective
   or Native Language Aptitude Differences?" *Modern Language Journal* 75 (1991): 3–16.

Sparks, Richard L., Leonore Ganschow, Silvia Kenneweg, and Karen Miller. "Use of an Orton-
   Gillingham Approach to Teach a Foreign Language to Dyslexic/LD Students: Explicit
   Teaching of Phonology in a Second Language." *Annals of Dyslexia* 41 (1991): 97–118.

Sparks, Richard L., Leonore Ganschow, and Jane Pohlman. "Linguistic Coding Deficits in Foreign Language Learners." *Annals of Dyslexia* 39 (1989): 179–95.

Sparks, Richard L., Jon Patton, Leonore Ganschow, Nancy Humbach, and James Javorsky.
   "Native Language Predictors of Foreign Language Proficiency and Foreign Language
   Aptitude." *Annals of Dyslexia* 56 (2006): 129–60.

Sparks, Richard L., Elke Schneider, and Leonore Ganschow. "Teaching Foreign (Second) Language to At-Risk Learners." In *Literacy and the Second Language Learner*, edited by JoAnn
   Hammadou Sullivan, 55–83. Greenwich, CT: Information Age, 2002.

Steele, Ross. *When in France, Do as the French Do: The Clued-In Guide to French Life, Language, and Culture.* Chicago, IL: McGraw-Hill, 2002.

Thompson, William Forde, E. Glenn Schellenberg, and Gabriela Husain. "Decoding Speech Prosody: Do Music Lessons Help?" *Emotion* 4 (2004): 46–64.

———. "Perceiving Prosody in Speech: Effects of Music Lessons." *Annals of the New York Academy of Sciences* 999 (2003): 530–32.

Vandergrift, Larry. "It Was Nice to See That Our Predictions Were Right: Developing Metacognition in L2 Listening Comprehension." *Canadian Modern Language Review* 58, no. 4 (2002): 557, 559.

Vogel, Susan, Yona Leyser, Sharon Wyland, and Andrew Brulle. "Students with Learning Disabilities in Higher Education: Faculty Attitude and Practices." *Learning Disabilities Research and Practice* 14, no. 3 (1999): 173–86.

Weinert, Franz E., and Rainer H. Kluwe. Introduction to *Metacognition, Motivation and Understanding*, edited by Franz E. Weinert and Rainer H. Kluwe, 121–39. Hillsdale, NJ: Lawrence Erlbaum Associates, 1987.

Wenden, Anita. "Metacognitive Knowledge and Language Learning." *Applied Linguistics* 19 (1998): 515–37.

Winograd, Peter, and Victoria Chou Hare. "Direct Instruction of Reading Comprehension Strategies: The Nature of Teacher Explanation." In *Learning and Study Strategies: Issues in Assessment, Instruction, and Evaluation*, edited by Claire E. Weinstein and Ernest T. Goetz, 121–39. San Diego, CA: Academic Press, 1988.

Young, Carissa, and Fong Yoke Sim. "Learner Diaries as a Tool to Heighten Chinese Students' Metacognitive Awareness of English Learning." In *Teaching English to Students from China*, edited by Gek Ling Lee, 21–34. Singapore: Singapore University Press, 2003.

Zimmerman, Barry J., and Albert Bandura. "Impact of Self-Regulatory Influences on Writing Course Attainment." *American Educational Research Journal* 31, no. 4 (1994): 845–62.

Index

CPSIA information can be obtained
at www.ICGtesting.com
Printed in the USA
LVHW050610231218
601452LV00007B/328/P